MUDFLAP

MUDFLAP

A true story ...

every little bit.

JAY ALDEN BAILEY

575 Main Street Press

www.mudflapthehero.com

Library of Congress Card Catalogue Number upon request.

ISBN-13: 978-1-7337465-1-9

575 Main Street Press
New Hartford, CT 06057

The Character *Mudflap*

The Author Jay Alden Bailey of New Hartford, Connecticut,
proclaims his character Mudflap by definition is:

A person who puts his or her own interest below that of another in selfless acts, taking the blame or responsibility for that person, and ends up under the proverbial bus.

Dedication

This book was finished on February 14th 2019 and is
dedicated to my first love.

Happy Valentine's Day to Gina Forline.

Like a shooting star, so beautiful and so brief.

Content

Chapter 1 The Development of Empathy
      1 The Beginning
      2 A New Beginning
      3 Moving Up
      4 1970
      5 The Neighborhood Matures
      6 Big Guy Now
      7 High School

Chapter 2 The World of Work
      1 Free at Last?
      2 The Last two Straws
      3 At the Doorstep

Chapter 3 Self Employed
      1 Up the Proverbial Ladder

Chapter 4 The Proverbial Ladder Breaks
      1 The Reversal
      2 Throw That Ladder Away

Chapter 5 The Great Maine Adventure
      1 A Fresh Start
      2 Choose a Direction
      3 Back and Forth
      4 Something's Got to Give

Chapter 6 A New Town a New Life
      1 Pay Back
      2 The Happy Time
      3 Reality Check

Chapter 7 Things Level Out

1 Flatlander
2 Family Time

Chapter 8 Year 2000
        1 Times Change
        2 The First Decade
        3 The Death of the Debt Monster
        4 The Monsters Debris Field

Chapter 9 Islands Only
        1 Pine
        2 Phoebe

Chapter 10 The Teens and Beyond
        1 New Hartford
        2 The Road of Life
        3 The Quiet Time Part 2
        4 Spirals and Circles
        5 The Troll Under the Bridge
        6 The Boy
        7 The Boy Part 2

Chapter 11 End Game
        1 The Fallout
        2 Bullies
        3 Wrap Up

Editor's Note

The editor does not claim any expertise or credentials in using this title but relied heavily on previous job experience assisting an editor. A big debt of gratitude is owed to our "ghost editor" who was of great assistance with the grammar and punctuation.

The reader may note some irregularities in regard to the positioning of exclamation points, etc. This is at the direction of the author. All words are his; very little editing was done in this regard.

Preface

    As Mudflap's story unfolds, I will point out mileposts in time that you may remember, or have heard of. Mudflap will make observations along the way. His feelings at different intervals may come to light, as well as his opinions and philosophy on different subjects.

    An observation or thought which may seem somewhat obscure at the time will tie in or set the stage for a point in the story.

    Many of these observations or thoughts are there to inspire you. Some are there to simply make you laugh.

    Parts of the story are not happy at all, and the humor may be dark as well. But to laugh in the face of adversity is sometimes the only way one can cope with the situation.

    Be patient if Mudflap goes off subject for a bit, he usually comes around to a point in the story.

    Mudflap will be quick to tell you, nice stories are not very interesting.

    Enjoy !

MUDFLAP

INTRODUCTION

Mudflap is the nickname of a person who puts his or her own interest below that of another in selfless acts, taking the blame or responsibility and ends up under the proverbial bus.

Mudflap is not necessarily under the wheels, but is hanging tight under that bus, taking all the dirt for the other person for extended periods of time.

Mudflap's spirit spans time from the beginning of humanity, and its symbol is as Americana as Abraham Lincoln and Mom's Apple Pie.

There is no end to the lengths Mudflaps are willing to go for the people in their lives who they care about. The empathy they have for others can outweigh that of their own. Many times they are blinded by the feeling that the person they help actually feels the same way in return.

There are often great rewards brought on by the simple Karma of these selfless acts.

But there is also great sorrow brought on by the interaction with human nature itself.

Mudflap is the story of many, but this particular story was inspired by the parent of a Millennial who took sixty years to realize who he really is, and his place in life, in family, and in society.

Quotes Inspiring the Author

My Daughter Alexandra: "No matter what you do, you are always under the bus."

David Attenborough in the series *Life*: "A parent's purpose is to pass on genes, and then insure the survival of the next generation."

From the Author

Sit back and relate, reflect and hopefully be inspired. Come under the bus with Mudflap.

Prologue

The jeep idles up to the dam; it is just after 3 a.m. He swings the nose into the center of the road and stops. Looking back, he flashes his spotlight quickly, and catches a glimpse of the trail, snaps off the light, dropping it on the passenger's seat, as he starts backing up.

When he feels far enough in off the road he turns off the engine. He sits there for a few minutes letting his eyes adjust to the darkness. The peepers are making a racket, breaking the still night.

He waits there, only the sound of the peepers and his heart beating, now more quickly. He reaches into his jacket and pulls out the half pint of whiskey he has brought along to shake off the chill of the night air, and to calm his nerves.

The whiskey feels good, it sends a little warm shiver up his spine. He sits back and relaxes, and takes another whack off the bottle. There is no hurry. Sitting there in the night he thinks about all the neighbors, sleeping, completely unaware of what is going to happen.

He had tried last week to open the gate on the dam; the thing was rusted shut. The gate had not been opened for years. He was through playing around being nice to the neighbors. They expected him to pay for everything, and they got to use the lake for nothing. He wanted everybody to help keep the lake nice and put in beaches.

Cheap bunch of bastards was his opinion. He was out to show them a lesson.

He takes another whack off the bottle, and reaches back and grabs the backpack from behind the passenger's seat. There is a pre-wrapped bundle of dynamite, all set to go with plenty of wire.

Time to get serious. He hops out, stands up and stretches. He finishes off the bottle, tossing it into the bushes. His heart is beating faster now. The calming effect of the whisky is gone, being replaced rapidly by adrenaline.

He carefully lays out the wire so it feeds easily towards the lake, and back to the jeep. He takes the detonator switch out of the backpack and slides it under the front seat, making sure everything is in order before he goes into the water.

The whole lake is no more than eight feet deep, ten at the dam. He knows exactly where the gate is. He can find it in his sleep. There is a rock wrapped up with the bundle of dynamite; it will stay put. He had already put a couple of rocks in the corner of the gate; all he has to do is drop it in place.

He slips into the water slowly, does not even make a splash. Making sure the wires are not caught, and giving it plenty of slack, he stops.

He listens to the peepers, tries to calm down and catch his breath. He takes three deep breaths, then in he goes. He has the steps counted perfectly; the weight of the bundle helps him go down. He is right on the spot, drops it in place and is back to the surface with plenty of air to spare.

Making his way up to shore, he locates the wire and takes up the slack as he heads back to the jeep. Now his heart is really pounding as he wraps the wire around the bumper a couple of times, and feeds the rest into the jeep.

Opening the door, and getting the switch out from under the seat, as fast as he can, he makes the connection to the box. He gets the wire tucked in behind the driver's seat and puts the switch in first, now moving slower and much more carefully.

He gets in and starts the engine, leaving the door open. He hesitates, enjoying the rush of the moment. Then he turns the switch, a rumble of thunder, the ground beneath the jeep shakes.

A split second of only the sound of the idling motor, then he hears the rush of water clearly above the sound of the engine.

He closes the door and pulls out onto the dark road, flips on the headlights, and laughs.

"That will fix them," he says to himself, and has to control the urge to speed as he goes down the road home.

MUDFLAP

Chapter 1

The Development of Empathy

The Beginning

Mudflap was born into a silver-spooned world of the post-World War II era. He was the second child of a third marriage, and the last of six children to be born to a philandering father who blamed his failed marriages on the social change of the times with women having more liberated lives and views, and as he put it, "harder to get along with."

His parents were very well off. His father was a real estate mogul who had residences in Connecticut and Florida in the 1950's before its common popularity we know today.

Mudflap's memories began very early and many stayed with him throughout his life. When he later questioned his own son about his memories he had little or no recollection at all. It led Mudflap to ponder whether the bliss of his son's childhood left him no markers which could enable him to recall the wonderful times he enjoyed, and those experiences so important to his development.

Even though his time in a blissful childhood was cut short, Mudflap remembered his home in Portland, Connecticut, and being at the home in Ft. Lauderdale, Florida, too. He worked out with his mother to the TV and Jack LaLane, enjoyed the pool and neighborhood in Florida as well as the more murky memories of Connecticut.

One time in Florida he was playing monster, putting a square, flat-bottomed waste basket on top of his head and walking around with his arms stuck out. He walked right into the pool – SPLASH! Somehow he could see his father take the time to roll up his sleeves and kneel down. OUT HE CAME WITH A SQUISH OF WATER IN HIS SNEAKERS AS HE HIT THE CEMENT! He looked over at his brother busy saving the basket with the cleaning net on a pole.

Then still in Florida, one day he went golfing with his father and brother, remembers having his toy set of plastic golf clubs with him. He was never to return. Mudflap and his brother were kidnapped by their father as pawns in what was to be a vicious divorce.

He was held captive in Meriden, Connecticut, by a lady friend of his father's who he will always remember as Flavia. The boys were told their mother was dead. They were lost for a time.

A frantic search for the boys was unfruitful, until one day a lady at the local bar who pretended to be drunk, but who was in the know, listened into the father's conversation and found out about the boys' location. She contacted their mother and the boys were rescued.

They ended up in an orphanage called the Curtis Home in Meriden until the authorities could figure out who was telling the truth, and who should have custody of the boys.

The Curtis Home was scary for Mudflap. Even at such a young age he was aware of time.

Finally they were reunited with their mother and moved to Durham, Connecticut, as penniless as their father could possibly make them. He had the time to cash out all the assets possible leaving a mess of the residual land mass of over 500 acres he had in his control in the Great Hill Pond, Portland area, that took the next 40 years to straighten out, and still to this day there are glitches in the land records.

The boys and their mother were alone as outcasts from the church and cousins of the strict Irish Catholic family. Only the mother's two brothers and sister, a paternal aunt and grandmother would have anything to do with them. The mother's parents were already dead and gone.

Mudflap was entering a different world as his childhood development took a whole new turn.

A New Beginning

Mudflap, now with his mother and brother in Durham, started his new life on the second floor of a cheap rental house, literally between the fork of two state highways, at the tender age of 3 years old. It was a sharp contrast from the serene upscale Floridian neighborhood, and the quiet lake house in the woods of Connecticut.

Tractor trailers hauled by the house at top speed, headed towards New Haven, because Interstate 95 had not yet been completed.

Mudflap was happy to be back with his mom, and despite all the upheaval, he adjusted quickly to his new environment. He loved to play in the large triangle of grass between the highways which was tightly packed with dandelions. They are such a perfect flower for a child to play in and with, and throughout his life he always reflected on the time he spent there, and cringed at the fact that they are such a widely despised flower.

His mother stayed home with him every day, because at that time there was no preschool at all in Durham before first grade. The ability to stay home was due largely to the support of her sister, who would continue to be of great help throughout the boys' childhood.

Mudflap was happy. Roy Rogers, Sky King, and the Chipmunks were all the rage. But his brother, three and a half years older, and much more aware of their father's absence, was not as well-adjusted. His body type was taller, his arms longer, and combined with his advanced age, Mudflap was no match for him physically. With anger building higher and higher as the time passed, Mudflap would become the target of his frustration throughout their childhood and into their adult lives. And, sadly, his brother would take that frustration to his grave.

The boys' mom had a very outgoing personality, and she quickly became friends with the people on the first floor, the neighbors up the hill in back, and the family who ran The Durham Inn, a quarter mile down the New Haven Road. They all became extended family, and despite the past, mom looked forward to doing the best she could to fulfill the role of both parents.

One day in the bitter cold the mom found a dog curled up in the leaves next to the house. No collar, a fully grown dog with long, white and black fur. Like what happened to them, it was alone and abandoned. The mom barely had enough money to feed the boys, let alone another mouth, but how could she not take the dog in. She was truly sent to them. "Susie" they named her, and she became a fearless protector of the family, an absolute pillar of their lives. As time evolved, so did her name and legendary status.   She became The Suzer and The Poozer named after the Perilous Poozers of Pompelmoose Pass. Suzer lived an extremely long life, almost till Mudflap was twenty years old. Since she was fully grown when they got her, he never really knew just how old she really was.

Moving up

Mudflap grew, he went to school, his mom to work, life moved on. There were many happy times, although the country had been going through a lot during this period that was not so happy.

He, along with the rest of the nation, had to deal with the shock of Kennedy's assassination. There was no Sky King or Roy Rogers, only that casket on the caisson rolling down the street on the few channels that existed, which lasted for days and days it seemed, at least in the mind's eye of a child. LBJ versus Goldwater, the sixties were starting to really fire up. Mudflap was acutely aware of the stress the adults around him faced.

One day a package came in a large manila envelope. Mom quickly opened it up. It was full of packing material, this old fashioned, pre- packing worms stuff, a blue kinda wool with colored strands in it. She pulled out the packing and as she got to the bottom she threw it to the floor and started to cry. The father had sent a package full of nothing.

Being in Florida in the early sixties, there were no dead-beat dad laws to protect them. They were on their own, couldn't get a dime out of their father, and he was rubbing her nose in it.

Mudflap learned how the extended families worked together to help and comfort each other; they were not really alone.

There were three children of the family at the inn, two boys older than Mudflap and one girl younger. He learned how to love outside of the immediate family circle.

One day the mom came in all excited about a new kind of treat she had found at the store: a Dannon Yogurt. She opened it up and the older brother took the first taste. He spit it out and cried out how horrible and sour it was. Her elation was flattened, her countenance a crushed painful look. Mudflap took the next taste. It was sour, but kinda sweet, too, a bit. Mudflap lied and said it was great and he wanted more. He could not bear to see his mom hurt. Over time he acquired a taste for it and ended up really loving it. She was ahead of the times, we all know where yogurt has gone from there. Mudflap misses the old wax cardboard container and that extra sour bite. (They call the taste Greek Yogurt today.)

First grade was a good experience. Mudflap had fun and liked it very much.

Whenever they went shopping for food, the mom would take out this little red plastic, hold-in-your-palm counter with three little white keys to punch.   As she went along, every item put in the carriage was priced and kept track of. When she reached her budget she stopped shopping. She often would squeeze out an extra bit of change to buy Mudflap a matchbox toy car or small treat. This simple counter would forever motivate Mudflap to work harder so his family could eat whatever they needed, regardless of cost. Once he even got a Beatle wig. Yes, the Beatles were here and we were all starting to rock and roll.

Back at school, second grade was not so fun as the first; Mudflap struggled. During that year the aunt helped the family move into a house at the far south end of town, in a modest neighborhood off the New Haven Road. It was safer with lots of other kids to interact with. The family who lived over the inn moved that way too - only a mile away - an easy walk for kids of the time. The couple on the first floor got a new house, too and the old couple on the hill in back retired to New Mexico; nobody was left behind. Life seemed to be getting better for everybody.

As they moved into their new home, a new person popped up in the boys' lives: the employer of the mom, who they at first were told to call uncle. He was an inventor of machine tools and had a small factory in Rockfall, about 12 miles away. The mom was his secretary; he was a really good guy. He was cozying up to the mother in an innocent sort of way it seemed. He was older, her boss, he liked his drinks, smoked, and was married. Maybe he would not have done so well today in the corporate work place.

This nice guy, who had a grown daughter from his current marriage, was somehow infatuated by the innocence of this cute family of three (and two boys he never had) who seemed to need saving. He was getting way in over his head, biting off more than he could chew, and so on. He was about to become a Big Time Mudflap, nice guy that he was. In retrospect, he would have lived a lot longer staying home.

It was not that long before uncle became a dad. There was a big wedding party at the aunt's house, (took the pressure off her), everybody liked him. Next thing you know, he was walking Suzer every morning on his so-called constitutionals.

Mudflap had to have been at least eight by then, the two-family house was fading away fast into the past.

Then one day the father showed up for a visit in an Indianapolis 500 Pace Car. It was a white Eldorado Convertible with a red interior, all the pace car decals still on the doors, flags all around, the works. The trunk was full of cigarettes and alcohol, duty free from South of the Border (The Carolinas). He wanted to meet the new husband and had party gifts for all.

He had come up once or twice before, always to show off. He did have a very nice new wife (number four) who Mudflap liked very much. She was always very kind to him and very beautiful. It was always a whirlwind of a visit. They all had to drop everything and pay attention to him. And there always was a very expensive dinner he would take the boys out to, because the mom sure was not going to have him at her table.

Mudflap was no chump, he knew how hard they had it through the years; the over-priced dinners didn't impress him in the least. His father would snap his fingers at the waitresses and make them hop around. Then in the end, if they snapped to it enough, he would tip them big and be sure to let everybody know.

The boys were growing up, big brother was approaching his teens, the sixties in full swing, times were escalating, and so was the violent behavior of the older boy. The common sibling rivalry and banter were starting to take a more aggressive turn.

And to make matters worse, Mudflap didn't like school. The teachers in second and third grade were these cranky old ladies that were really mean. The third grade teacher was a nasty old thing with tight curly white hair, big pearl necklace and cameo earrings. She jacked up poor little Mudflap in the hall, like the coach of a football team gone wild. The fourth grade teacher was a nicer old gal, but disillusioned by Mudflap's lack of attention. She would put on these math tests with time limits and Mudflap could not stop watching the clock; he just couldn't concentrate. Then she would always call on him and put him on the spot. The fifth grade old lady was a nightmare for real! Mudflap couldn't understand where they got all these witches. By the sixth grade they started to split up the classes into four rooms. You got a home room, then moved around, finally some guy teachers. But the old English teacher was another witch of a nightmare; she hated Mudflap. He was pretty much a C student with an occasional B and a lot more D's. Finally, one quarter on a report card, the English teacher gave Mudflap an F in spelling. She harangued him about where he was going to go in the world without being able to spell. Mudflap thought for a moment then replied, "I will have a secretary."

Made sense to him, his mother was a secretary, and his father had a secretary. The look the lady gave him told Mudflap she wanted to kill him. If he had only known, he could have thrown spell check at her too.

Every day he couldn't wait to get out of school and go out into the woods and swamps to play. He loved turtles and frogs, snakes and every little creature he could find. He and Suzer would get lost in the woods for hours at a time; they were best friends. Totoket Mountain was behind their house, and there were endless miles of woods to explore. The fork in the road at the two-family house, where he played in the dandelions at three years old, were the same roads that surrounded the mountain. By the end of his run in Durham, Mudflap knew most all the woods in town.

1970

The Teenage Years, Rock and Roll, Flower Power's Gone

It's not about the Revolution, it's about the Party

Hold onto your Hats - Everything is a Go

(The Woods are the only Stable Place)

Mudflap turns twelve and things have been changing. His love of the woods and environment are the only things that have any deep meaning. The rest is happening so fast; nobody is ahead of the curve.

The stepfather and mom were preoccupied with their work. We can all relate to that in the new millennium, because nobody gets a break in mainstream America today. It was all about their business, their relationship, paying the bills as responsible parents, and coming home at night and unwinding.

But who's watching the children at Mudflap's house in 1970?

Nobody, that was the problem.

And nobody knew were the first cousin was.

The mom's brother lost his son. For the longest time nobody knew what happened to him.

He finally emerged from under the staircase at

Mudflap's house, after living there for two weeks. Mudflap's brother had been hiding him and feeding him on the sly. He must have come out at night and when everybody was at work and school. He had problems due to divorced parents and not acclimating into either new marriage situation. But for good, bad or indifferent reasons he ended up as Mudflap's other brother (his big cousin). He came to live with them for the next couple of years until he graduated from high school. They were no strangers to extended family; they all hung tight.

Mudflap was just twelve, but his siblings were three and a half and four and a half years older. With no parental control after school, things were going faster than anyone could keep up with.

The neighborhood they moved to did have lots of kids. It was a great dynamic to grow up in. The road was a dead end so it was like its own eco-system. Many close relationships developed. The biggest yard, open and central to the neighborhood, ended up designated as the football field. It was not a place for the faint of heart. They all played a tough game, and of course there was no safety equipment. Often kids would go home crying, but it would not be long before they would return, ready for some pay back. The owner of the football field never gave a thought to any legal repercussions. No neighbor at the time would even think to sue over scrapes and bangs. I can't imagine anyone these days ever dreaming of taking on that kind of liability.

There was a designated part of the road for baseball too. Hard ball, of course. Maybe not quite a contact sport, but it could be a lot more dangerous. They tried to play by the rules, but line drives and flying bats caused casualties.

There was an age split in the hierarchy of the neighborhood. The Big Kids and the Little Kids. As far as the games went, anyone willing to play and take a team position was welcome. Each game was set up, team members picked, with an attempt at fair play and to ensure a good game.

There was no basketball court. Mudflap took it upon himself to chop down a tree with an axe. He dug a hole in the perfect spot in front of his house on the sharpest curve in the road. With help they installed the backboard and rim and erected the set up. With painted lines, the sports center was complete. It was not the contact sport like football, no flying objects other than the ball itself, but the game had a sort of hockey style to it, with checks and flying elbows.

Mudflap's brother especially liked using his elbows, and Mudflap was always sure to get more than his fair share.

As the relationship between the mom and her boss grew, she spent more time at the office and out to dinner at night. Once married, the hours didn't get any shorter. They were really into running their machine tool business, he the inventor, she the outgoing customer service person and his personal secretary too. Nobody was starving at home for food but discipline was being dispensed by big brother. Torture was dispensed more out of boredom than corporal punishment. He was creative in the ways punishment was dealt out. Any reason was a good reason to strike. With those longer arms, a punch was almost completely unavoidable. And he began to like blood - a shot to the nose or mouth was a sure way to get a splash. Some evenings the parents got home late, sometimes they would come home and decide to go back out for dinner, most likely thinking mom deserved a break not having to cook. Mudflap would beg them not to leave him there to be tortured. The brother would assure them Mudflap was in good hands and glance back over his shoulder at him with a menacing smile.

By the time big cousin moved in everyone was pretty comfortable living in the new neighborhood. Cousin fit in well and gained high status as biggest of the big kids. Mudflap was about to enter middle school. With the household basically under the control of the big kids during the hours after school, it was the go-to place for everyone around to escape parental controls. Although Mudflap was a little kid, he was caught up in the big kids' world. The party was starting to kick into gear.

The parents liked their cocktails after a long day, as did the other parents in the neighborhood. Block parties and beer were not uncommon. There was no police department in the small cow town of Durham, so resident state troopers were the norm. The small street of about twenty-two houses had two resident troopers living there, one right next door to

Mudflap. In retrospect, one would have to admire the fact that never once in all the years that followed did he ever come over and say one word at all. He came home and kept to himself, despite the next four to five years of teenage drivers coming and going. Late, loud music parties, people from other neighborhoods and later towns, muscle cars, motorcycles, fights, screaming. We are talking years, and not a peep out of him. Everyone in the know was comfortable seeing the state cruiser just shy of the basketball court, right in front of Mudflap's house. On occasion visitors would tear off and zoom away upon arrival, thinking there was a bust going on.

But we were all as safe as could be, the 70's were here, and everything was a go!

The Neighborhood Matures

Mudflap at twelve had now been in the woods and swamps for years and considered himself an authority on the native reptiles and amphibians. Snakes, being the most feared, gave him prestige in his ability to catch and contain such creatures. He had already established a long history of events like making boats out of boxes wrapped with plastic, and floating them into snake and snapping turtle-infested old farm ponds, taking innocent friends with him, risking all for that next big catch.

There was a very large old oak tree behind the houses. Mudflap and his closest friends in the little kids circle built a three-level tree fort. It was a real sketchy setup, the top level a lot higher than small children with no training in carpentry should be building. And with junk materials. It was amazing what they got away with. Also, these small kids were going way up into the woods; there were absolutely miles of forest back there. Climbing up waterfalls, or exploring deserted hermit shacks, there were endless places to get yourself in trouble out there.

Back by the houses, the games and general horsing around were always on the wild side. Nobody leashed their dogs and most everybody had one. Dog fights were common and always a great source of excitement. As in the woods, Suzer could hold her own. But still, it was all rather on the innocent side.

Mudflap was already getting a bad reputation with some of the more coddling mothers as one your child should not hang around with. All things pass, and time advances, his life with reptiles in the forefront was coming to a close, and the world of the big kids was coming to take precedence.

How do you tell your kids not to do something when you do it?

Like drinking and smoking. Today, smokers are shunned. But back then Walter Cronkite did it on the news. The kids caught on quickly that the easiest source for contraband was the parents. Mudflap had been for his whole life going around putting out the burning cigarettes left going by his mom. Little burnt worm marks were all over the tables around the house. She and her new husband were bookworms, smoking all the while they were reading.

They also liked their mixed drinks. The bar was full of all sorts of different types of liquor. The big kids started drinking, so of course Mudflap followed suit soon after.

The new dad was an old-fashioned, Waspy New Englander, quirky inventor, Eagle Scout (back when it was really hard to be an Eagle), fiscally-tight kinda guy, who drove a Rambler. The kinda guy who would be in his Rambler getting in the way of a huge trailer truck and not budging because he has the right of way. Almost a Mr. Magoo sort of character, oblivious to things around him and off in his own little world.

He was the complete opposite of Mudflap's father, who was a reckless, self-absorbed real estate salesman driving the pace car with extravagant spending habits.

The poor old guy never saw it coming. Only when the liquor started getting watered down, and it affected his cocktail and buzz, did he start to realize what was going on, then he was mad. Lesson #1: don't water down the booze! You could steal a lot cause they really had trouble keeping track, but water, that was realized fast.

Then the parents started locking up the cabinet. The game was on! The boys picked the lock. Now you had more people wanting the alcohol than there was available. Competition got tight.

There were threats of repercussions if break-ins were caught. Didn't stop anybody, it just got a lot of finger pointing.

Then there was the little travel bar suitcase item. Mudflap figured out how to tap out the hinges with a finishing nail, always an easy hit.

The Boys were just warming up.

All this activity was not helping anybody at school. Mudflap liked school - it was the bookwork that was the problem. The other activities and the social interaction were fun. That mean sixth-grade English teacher moved up to the new middle school too. She continued to harass him for the whole next year.

The school bus was a horrible place too: noise, fights broke out, and there was a time they went through drivers like socks. Mudflap hated the bus ride so much he only took it home. Every morning he started to wait in the woods until it left, and then he would hitchhike in. The state highway had its advantages. Mostly he got a ride from a commuting male teacher who wouldn't drive by him. They became friends.

The older boys started bring pot home. The genie was out of the bottle.

The fights between Mudflap and his brother kept escalating. Mudflap was getting better at his defenses, which made it a lot less fun for his brother. The brother was a poor sport and didn't like to lose any game, the fight one especially. It was not beneath him to attack by surprise from behind if he felt Mudflap had done too well in the last fight.

Mudflap's bedroom had a window to the garage roof that was very convenient for exits, as well as the brazen act of sitting on the peak of the roof with lawn chairs, drinking.

Mudflap lost his virginity with the help of a friend who had a line on a couple of girls a neighborhood over.

Mudflap still found time to hike in the woods, but now there were pot and beer parties in the woods too. He was a boy scout and camper but they were a wild bunch.

The cousin was a smart guy and helped more than hurt, but nobody was a saint.

The brother started driving and bringing home more of his sketchy friends.

The new dad got the idea to turn the garage into a work shop-recreational room sort of thing. Took out the roll up door and put in a wall with a picture window. They got a ping pong table. Everyone got very good at it, and it became very competitive. Of course ping beer started, that was fun. Mudflap was getting bigger and starting to catch up physically. He started beating his brother in ping pong. It can be a very aggressive game and of course a picture window was not the best idea for that format. In the heat of the moment, at the losing volley, Mudflap's brother could not control his temper and that paddle would fly, Mudflap would duck, and there would go the window.

Time was passing, the cousin graduated and worked at the machine tool shop in the drafting department a bit. There were some big parties. Mudflap's brother thought he was on TV in a bar fight - his temper so bad he would trash the house - using chairs as clubs, and throwing things into mirrors. He was out of control when he didn't get his way, and this is only the short version. The fights were just knock-down, drag-them-out bloody.

Then one day it finally came to a head for Mudflap. After his brother threw the paddle into the picture window for a third time, he knew he was in trouble because the parents were really fed up. He came at Mudflap with a serious vengeance and was going nuts. He knocked Mudflap to the floor and was kicking him in the face. Mudflap struggled to get up, managing to stop his foot in mid-swing, and got a hold of his balls, giving them a good yank. He was kneed back to the floor and received a few more kicks before the ball squeeze pain finally kicked in. In a blur, Mudflap could see him bending over holding his groin. Mudflap stood up, staggering a bit like being drunk, but with clear recollection of that foot coming at his face. Luckily for Mudflap his brother was wearing sneakers, but Mudflap had on boots. He stepped back and got his bearings, brother still bent over. With a full concentrated swing, he kicked him in the face and lifted him right off the ground. He was knocked back to the floor and Mudflap, for the first time, was in the position to really finish him off and win this fight. He stood there for a moment and just looked at him, helpless on the floor. Then Mudflap realized that he didn't have the same amount of anger in him as his brother did; he could never really win this way. He just did not have it in him. It was not the last fight, but Mudflap knew he had won forever.

Bad things happening to good people has always contradicted karma. The nicest people of them all, the original friends from the inn, were not in the neighborhood but close by down the New Haven Road. They were a tight, unbroken family who did not carry on like Mudflap's household. Their daughter, the sweetest thing ever, developed brain cancer, and her death ripped those poor people's hearts out. Her dad, one of the toughest guys Mudflap knew, was brought to his knees. Seeing that guy crying in church was the most painful experience Mudflap ever had. It's much too painful a story to go on about, but it couldn't be left out. Later in life, one of the boys, Mudflap's brother's close friend and the same age, died too. He had some kinda gambling problem and Mudflap always wondered if he felt life was just a crap shoot.

Innocence gone, Mudflap was going into his last couple years of high school. He didn't feel like a kid anymore, he was a battle-hardened, tough guy looking for a good time. The last couple years of high school would fit the bill well.

A Big Guy Now

Mudflap was ending his sophomore year in the new regional high school for Durham and Middlefield. He had watched it being built while he was in the elementary school during grades four through six across the street. They turned the old high school into the middle school and now the town had a complex of buildings and sports fields. The merger brought a whole new group of kids from Middlefield, making for a more interesting social dynamic.

Motorcycles caught his attention as he had friends who could afford them and he had a chance to ride a couple. He became friends with one of the big kids at the bottom of his neighborhood. They were hard-drinking buddies. This kid was a real "Gear Head," as they were called back then, as opposed to the "Freaks" who were the long-haired potheads. His Gear Head buddy always had projects going on. (which Mudflap got into, and still to this day, projects overwhelm Mudflap's life.) There were piles of junk cars around his buddy's house, testing the patience of the other neighborhood state trooper who lived next door.

That trooper was quite the character. At one point, the kids would see him go off to work in the morning while they were at the bus stop. He was dressed up in leathers and a beard as an undercover cop in New Haven. There were stories of his exploits as a super cop who would even dive off piers to chase down his perpetrator. We all loved him, and thought he was the coolest guy around.

As time passed the "Gear Head" became known as "Crazy Man" because of his super fast, new 750 two-cycle Kawasaki with expansion chamber exhaust that made an unbelievably loud noise. He would tear out of the street, front end bouncing. There was a perfect, quarter-mile straight-away close by for drag races and you could hear him going for miles. If you remember, there was not a lot going on back then for entertainment. Even the TVs were limited and you needed to have skill in just adjusting the channels. Everyone was dirt poor (but didn't know it) with few material goods. Unlike today where there is just so much out there for everybody to have. So having a car or motorcycle was a really big thing.

Mudflap wanted wheels. His sixteenth birthday was approaching in the foreseeable future, but his parents laughed. There was no way he was getting a license the way he drank and carried on. They finally had leverage on him. Mudflap had to cool down to get what he wanted.

Mudflap's prior summers were spent at camps. Before eleven years old they were spent at the YMCA day camp. Then, entire six weeks at the scout camp. Those were great summers for him because of his love of the outdoors. And great summers for the parents, too, as it was worth every dime to get rid of him.

But this summer was to be different. He needed money for a car. His parents had no intention of helping him into one. His brother had already trashed the Buick, and then the Rambler. The abusive one got two cars and Mudflap got none. Didn't seem fair; he had to do something. His birthday was in September, nobody was going to hire him at fifteen. He had to lie about his age to get a job. He had to lie to be sixteen, so what was the difference if he lied to be eighteen? His hair was long, his build full - it wasn't a stretch by appearance. He landed a good-paying job in a factory. Only problem was, it was twelve miles away in Rockfall near his parents' shop, and it was third shift. But Mudflap had a plan.

Every night at 11 o'clock he rode his bike all the way to Rockfall, and in the morning he would put the bike in his mom's hatchback Pinto and hitchhike home. But first he would stop at the package store and buy a six-pack of Bud Kings for the hitchhike. Showing off the six-pack with his thumb out was a sure way to get a quick ride. He would drink a couple himself and give the rest to the driver, often getting a ride all the way home. It was a great system!

That summer he saved $900 and for the rest of his life he was never broke again. He would continue to buy, sell, and swap vehicles all the way to a fleet of equipment. Mudflap was on his way to being a responsible person.

High School

Always quick to get any project off to a good start, Mudflap started high school with a goal in mind. That was to get out of there as fast and easy as possible. He looked at the prerequisites for a diploma and filled up his schedule.

He took some bad advice and had algebra for a math class. Not for long. Homework was not his thing; he didn't like school cutting into his off time. He only would do homework at study hall. If there was no time at study there was no time at all, and algebra was a needy course. First test he knew absolutely nothing on it. He had no fear of the teachers so he got up and started to leave. When questioned where was he going, his reply was, "to drop your class."

At the guidance office, they didn't like his idea to take a business math course; it was too simplistic and was not college prep. Mudflap had no intention of going to college; he wanted out and into the work force ASAP. They wouldn't cooperate and had to have approval from his mom. She straightened them out fast, saying, "He is going to do whatever he wants so best advice I can give to you is just leave him alone." That set the tone for the next four years and guidance counselors from then on were not very nice to him. Even in today's schools the trades are viewed as substandard and college is pushed on everyone, regardless of a child's aptitude. This is part of a bigger problem in that colleges are more of an enterprise, the students are more like inventory, and the parents become the patsies; their savings and equity in their homes are put into the meat grinder to satisfy the greed of the corporate-style system the colleges have become. Thus making a larger problem for the whole country. Parents and kids alike are stuck with debts they struggle to pay off, many without the jobs promised by the advanced education they are paying for. A gap exists in the trades where contractors need help and can't find it, because the system has demonized the trades as for only the stupid.   This has been exacerbated by smart phones and the internet where kids need instant gratification and their attention spans have become that of gnats. The greed is only rivaled by the banking system, which drove down interest rates so low that the only way the general public can make any money to retire on is to be forced into a volatile stock market.

That's why we should as parents pay more attention to the long-term happiness of the children who may not want to be stuck in unsatisfying jobs, paying tribute to a system which cares nothing about them at all. Or cares nothing for the parents who have to work themselves till they drop.

Little old Mudflap was ahead of the curve way back in 1973. But that doesn't mean he was going to escape the tsunami of crap headed for everyone in the new millennium.

When Mudflap was a freshman, the social scene was very different from the way it would be when he graduated. It was a time when society was starting to think more out of the box. Trial and error techniques were applied at the schools. A smoking pit, as they called it, was instituted because the bathrooms were chaos. Mudflap would walk into a smoke-filled room with the upper classmen pitching quarters. It was very intimidating for any poor kid coming from a proper upbringing. Mudflap thought it was a hoot! Three kids at a time huddled around each toilet passing around cigarettes and often joints. Getting to a urinal was hard enough; nobody was taking a dump at school. When suddenly the door would crash open, there was a teacher, cigarettes dropped to the floor, toilets all flushed. Anyone caught with a cigarette in his hand was hauled away.

Combined with the regional mix of all the new kids, school was a blast. There were so many girls: some older ones decked out as if for a pageant show. It was a real zoo.

By the time he was a junior Mudflap had completed most of his prerequisite classes. All he needed for hard classes to graduate was US History and two more years of English. He was more of a humanities guy anyway so it was a piece of cake. Guidance scowled at him as he chose shop, art, chorus, and home economics. Home Ec. was great - he was the only guy and he got all the taste treats.

As much as he liked girls and with his beyond years experience, landing one was more of a challenge than you would think. Alcohol and wild parties took away inhibitions. Mudflap was a more sensitive guy than his tough appearance may have led one to believe. He really did like relationships and found the company of girls to be the best part of school, hands down. There are many he remembers and sometimes wonders how they made out in life.

In his senior year a new girl came into the school as a senior, too. Her father, who knew everything smart as he was, burnt their house down unthawing a window with a rolled up newspaper. He hesitated to call for help thinking he could control the fire as it went up the drapes. He most likely left Newington to save himself the embarrassment of being that guy who did such a deed.

Like a new rat in the cage all the guys swarmed her. Shallow as they were it was only because she was so strikingly beautiful. There was literally a line out the door of guys waiting for a spot at the table in the lunch room, just to get a chance to talk to her for a moment.

Mudflap wasn't waiting in line to talk to anybody. There were plenty of cute girls he had his eyes on. He actually avoided her. As human nature dictates, people in general want what they can't or don't have. Thus the story of Adam and Eve. The Bible has great wisdom, but why some take it so literally is a mystery. I know the world is more than 5000 years old and I hope the Rapture is not coming soon.

Eventually she found Mudflap, and once targeted, he was no match for her seductive powers. She was everything anyone would want in a love affair.

Mudflap was like a wild horse, who was now in

the corral and needed taming.

He had reached his goal of a car by taking two old Saab 96's and putting them together. He taught himself to weld, getting supplies from a new gas and welding supply company, walking distance from his house. It was a great accomplishment for him, but tragedy was about to strike. He was over at his buddy's house across town, hanging out like any typical evening. Coincidentally, (there is really no such thing as coincidences; it's all in the powers that be) his old neighbors from the 1st floor rental lived right across the street. It was pouring rain, and Mudflap found out the hard way why you want good tires on your car. He was going a bit too fast for the conditions on Main Street, passed the school, and hydroplaned off the road rolling the car into the river. He was saved most likely by a chain link fence that slowed him down, taking part of it with him into the water. Luckily, it was not too deep, and of course he had no seat belt on. Mudflap, in shock, scrambled out the passenger side window that was facing upwards. Got out, looked at the mess, and got back in to think about what he was going to tell everybody. The details of where he called from and who took him to the hospital for a checkup escape Mudflap today. He really was more bummed out about his car. He had taken bigger beatings from his brother.

Next he got a $75 special: a Chevy Biscayne Wagon. Back then, after 100,000 miles cars were put out on the road for anywhere from $50 to a $150. He would continue to go from one junk to another for awhile.

His friend from across town had more resources at his disposal and Mudflap got to ride around in his Oldsmobile 442. His friend was a fan of the "Crazy Man," and it was always an interesting ride. Mudflap had to keep both hands on the ceiling of the car to keep from smashing his head as they went over the bumps in the road. His friend had a couple of horses, too, which were fun to ride. They were always looking for excitement of some kind. He had another friend on the same side of town; the senior year was one escapade after another. Later, they were to be his motorcycle riding buddies.

Mudflap was the envy of all the guys in school having the Queen. But all long-term relationships need maintenance; anyone telling a different story is lying. Before the year was over, she had to go back to Newington to try out her new skills on the old boyfriend. It crushed Mudflap. During the next four years that followed in that on-again, off-again relationship, as much as he loved her, that original magic of those first months would be gone forever. After the final breakup, Mudflap would have to endure a decade of in-between relationships before finding the love of his life.

June of 1976 was the liberation Mudflap had been waiting for all these years.

And yes, Mrs. Vance, Mudflap does have a secretary, and there is spell check, too.

Chapter 2

The World of Work

Free at Last?

So there was Mudflap out of school, but what to do next? His on- and off-again relationship was on the cool side, so he really was not sure. Women have a way of doing that to a guy.

He had intuition for things, and throughout his life he would many times find himself ahead of the curve before things became in vogue. He had a knack for foreseeing things, or to put himself at the right place at the right time. This talent would prove to become of great value as a self-employed person.

Staying ahead of things in general is always good. Shedding skin like his friends the snakes, Mudflap changed rapidly. He quit smoking by the time he was sixteen, no longer as fun at the legal age. Back in his junior year at school, he noticed the teachers sporting longer hair, beards, mustaches; the sixties' look of rebellion was now the normal look of the seventies. By that third year of high school Mudflap's hair was down his back. Seeing the establishment conform to the rebellion made him cringe. Mudflap flipped his persona and cut all his hair off, the butch cut as it was called back then. Today, even getting your hair cut has changed. The barber shops have almost all but disappeared, replaced by salons. Back then, when you asked for a regular haircut, you got it cut around your ears and were left some bangs to comb over your forehead. They even gave you a little pocket comb to go home with. Today, when you ask for a regular haircut, you get a dumbfounded look. Everything has to be a special style. Mudflap had also ditched the alcohol in that junior year, noticing more of the goody two-shoe kids were beginning to indulge. Combined with a good woman to help straighten out his attitude, Mudflap was ready to work.

He realized this moment would be his only free one for a long time, because once he started working he would be sucked into the grind like his parents. Oh, how right he was!

Comfortable hitchhiking for years, he said good-by and left for the West Coast. The short story is he didn't make it past Arizona. Using youth hostels he had some fun, but the reality of travel with little money made it not quite the romantic journey he was seeking. And all that corn, he thought he would never get out of Kansas. As he crossed the Plains, he could see only heat waves in the distance. He started to see a mirage of sorts, something there in the heat waves; he kept staring at it. Only clouds, he started thinking. They got darker, a storm? The sky was full ahead, what the hell is that he thought, and finally realized it was the Rocky Mountains sticking right out of the Plains like a wall.

That was the best part. He spent the 4th of July in Denver. Tried to find the old couple who moved to New Mexico. He started meeting too many weird people, so he decided to head back east to Washington, DC, where his big cousin was living and working for the Washington Post.

His cousin landed a job at the Post when Katherine Graham fired everybody. He had to cross strike lines to go to work, but he wasn't afraid of a few strikers. Hell! He grew up at Mudflap's house.

His mother lived in Virginia, and everybody was very hospitable to Mudflap. The aunt put him up, loaned her car to Mudflap, the party was on. It was so fun he went back to Connecticut, got his things and came back in the Biscayne. He got a job at a construction site as a laborer. He was not afraid to start at the bottom, even started a bank account. But then something he was not used to happened: prejudice. He was "The Yankee Boy." At first he thought it was just a little fun banter, a guy thing. He came to realize quite quickly they were serious, and he wasn't going to get anywhere down there. So Mudflap said his thanks and goodbyes and went home.

People evolve. The "Crazy Man," a positive influence on Mudflap, was making a fortune for the standards of the time, doing piece work at the factory. Little Durham, the cow town, was also famous as a national "Metal Box King". There were Durham Manufacturing and two spin-off factories in town. The sister town of Middlefield, with the village of Rockfall, had lots of manufacturing going on as well.

Mudflap went through a series of factory-type jobs, not lasting long at any. He hated being inside, didn't know what his calling was yet, but knew being trapped indoors was not for him. In the last factory, workers got mad at him because he went too fast making them look bad. He was not allowed to make more money even at piece work. What was this place, he thought? It was like communism or something, all little drones. He wanted to stand out as an individual.

He had a job at Wesleyan University at the Physical Plant. It was a job for life, an easy ride. He was told how stupid he was for leaving. All they did was hide from work in the steam tunnels, and purposely did not teach him the trade to hold him down. One day at lunch, he was drinking a milkshake that he started to bring in because the acids in his stomach were burning a hole right through him. His eye caught parts of the old label on his used container. Three different spots of scrap label read NOT FOR U. He got up and started walking out. When questioned where he was going, he replied with a cocky comment somewhere in the same realm as his reply as he left the algebra test. When Mudflap is done, he's done.

Throughout all the entry-level, low-paying jobs, he did manage to buy the newest, fastest, production motorcycle on the market: a Kawasaki KZ 900. Motorcycles were the cleanest-cut activity, besides walking in the forest, Mudflap had. They mixed with the forest too. Dirt bikes, (enduro style, on/off road) were his first interest. They enabled him to go all over town through trails and road systems, and gave him valuable experience with small engines that would help him as a contractor in the future. Bikes gave him the thrills and joy he needed to offset those hard, low paying, depressing jobs he had to endure.

The friends from across town bought 900's too. They modified the exhausts, tweaked the engines and in the gearhead style born of the Greaser subculture of the fifties, Mudflap and friends carried on the American tradition of freedom on the wild side.

Little towns back then, with less social restrictions than higher-end suburban towns closer to cities, spawned some wild people. Their view of fun was a bit more of a twisted humor. The police didn't like dirt bikes on the road, and it was illegal to ride on the power line roads that cut through the woods for the high tension wires. These roads were often very rough and washed out so no cars could navigate them very far. It was fun to play cat and mouse with the cops, a dangerous game with consequences if you were caught. But that's what made the adrenaline flow. Mudflap loved adrenaline, it beat any drug for a thrill. That's why he cut trees, too. Durham, trying to modernize as the population grew, farms falling into the hands of developers, employed for the first time a constable. Gave him a jeep, and a little authority, and it went to his head.

Can't blame some poor old dairy farmer who worked cheap his whole life like a dog to take the offer of a million dollars to stop and have a normal life.

Mudflap admired the state troopers, and their respect for their neighbors and general public alike. It was still an innocent time when a cop would take your keys and drive you home if he caught you drunk driving. Obviously times change and they can't afford that liability anymore. The constable was petty, and deserved little respect. Mudflap and the gang easily out-maneuvered him on their dirt bikes. Later, one night in the big street bike phase, the constable thought he had the gang caught down at the high school complex. He chased them into the high school's dead end parking lot. It only led him to further frustration, as the guys knew the little escape trail that led to a road behind the school. They easily maneuvered their big bikes through the tight trail and made darn sure he heard those rocket engines scream away as each bike hit the pavement.

Another time Mudflap had to personally reprimand the constable. Mudflap and a couple friends were target practicing way up in the woods behind their houses. With a little more money now, recreation was getting more high tech, unlike playing with sticks. High caliber rifles cracked with that supersonic sound that made it so fun. Mudflap and company, as good old country boys, scouts and general all-around woodsmen, knew the safety rules and laws. They were acting responsibly, shooting into a hill a half mile away from any house. Army surplus ammunition could be bought cheap and they were firing up a storm. Somebody always has to complain. Mudflap was taking aim at the target, finger on the trigger. Looking through his sights, he sees movement, a bouncing action, an off color. The bouncing thing grew higher; it was a hat. He watched as the constable's head came into view. There was no trail back there. Mudflap thought, "what an idiot." He was sneaking through the bushes getting, right into the line of fire. Not very savvy.

Mudflap was a twitch away from taking his head off. Then he had the nerve to come over and threaten Mudflap with an arrest. Mudflap let loose with a sharp tongue that channeled his Irish-Catholic mother and aunt. Those ladies could rip you to shreds, leaving you crying and shaking without lifting a finger. They had a quick backhand too. He sent that constable home with his tail between his legs, telling him he was lucky to be alive, and if he pushed it further, he would soon be unemployed.

Mudflap has to this day always admired and respected the State Police. Where he resides now, resident state troopers still protect the small town. Retired troopers are the constables. These rural, small town police know how to cut a little slack to the public, showing them respect; and in return, gaining so much more respect themselves. They show compassion. These men should be considered role models for police around the nation. Maybe Mudflap can help the system realize that compassion is the way to fight back against the bad press police get in the media today.

Mudflap was back with his girl; that was a plus, but she had expensive taste and was use to being spoiled by her parents. She could spend a quarter of his week's pay being taken to dinner, which she liked very much and expected as often as possible.

Cutting trees became an option. Mudflap's brother worked for a small tree company and got him a job. He was again at the bottom working like a dog, cheap, but thinking he was working his way up the ladder. Mudflap always tried to mend the relationship with his brother - you fought, but you were still family no matter what.

The best thing about that tree job was it gave Mudflap hours behind a saw. I mean a lot of hours, clearing house lots. He would cut the road in, the driveways off and into the lots, then implode the lots. They worked like mad men. Back when Mudflap was still in school somebody built a house in the woods not far from his house. They cut the trees and filled in the swamp where he had played as a small child. He hated them for it. Now he was in the woods destroying it too. At times it bothered him, always aware of the little animals. He stayed in the lines and never cut any tree he didn't have to. Working hard didn't get him more pay.

A summer read Mudflap recently enjoyed: It was working with trees, but not what he was expecting. It had a significant moral to the story that should be applied to our entire work force at every level, office and trades alike. (The book: *Cutting Back* by Leslie Buck.)   The message that Mudflap got escapes many in our workforce today. The impeccable standards kept by the Japanese garden tree crew. These men were dedicated to discipline, quality, and determination to strive for the utmost perfection possible, even under the most adverse conditions. They respected the hierarchy of craftsmen above them, not only in their particular crew, but of the generations before them. The spirit of competition was to win, not just for one's ego, but for the good of the entire crew and well-being of all.

Mudflap enjoyed working like a mad man, and kept an impeccable standard in his own limited view of the standard of that time. He ended up out-producing his superiors. One day, in a frenzy, Mudflap was just going all out. There was finally room to drop the "Big One." Still relatively a beginner, he was not working with ropes - just a saw, a hammer, and wedge. (Without a line in a tree, if you don't have the balance correct, you can be in big trouble.) He was working alone; the other guys were on the next lot. The monster-sized oak with a wide spreading canopy was notched, back cut, the saw off, and Mudflap was slamming the wedge into the back cut. The cracks of the hammer like the sound of gun shots rang out. It woke up his superiors, they saw Mudflap behind the monster swinging the hammer. Seeing the size of the tree, they panicked, ran over and stopped Mudflap. They told him to get back. They stood under the tree, looking up and discussing it for what seemed a very long time. Mudflap couldn't hear what they were saying. He was starting to get mad watching them. Finally they called him back over and told him to proceed. At least they didn't take the drop away from him. They all watched as it fell perfectly to the ground.

At the end of the week, Mudflap asked for a raise he knew he deserved, but got nowhere. Feeling unappreciated, he quit.

There were two major business experiences Mudflap had that prepared him for his future.

The new welding supply and gas company down the street from Mudflap's house was a struggling business. Here, he would not only work cheap at an entry level pay, but would really extend himself to the owner, and put in time far surpassing what he would get paid for. He devoted more time to that job, more than any other he would ever hold in his life.

Mudflap knew the owner of the gas company because he had been a customer. The man was very seasoned in his industry. His age, and smooth-talking salesmanship, impressed Mudflap, and made him believe that there was a future in the company. Mudflap already understood the pecking order and the proverbial ladder. The fact that it was a chance at the number two spot seemed appealing.

At first the job entailed putting in store hours to free up the boss. Mudflap did get to go on deliveries, too, but had to spend a lot of hours inside a place that saw very little walk-in traffic. Gas grills were new. One job was filling propane tanks from a huge bulk tank. Mudflap learned about safety and maintenance, spending time painting old 100-pound tanks used by houses for stoves and water heaters. The job was too slow, but he kept looking at it from a future perspective.

The more time on the road, the happier Mudflap was. He learned more about welding equipment and was encouraged to stop and sell the service to garages, factories and fabricators along the way as he serviced existing customers.

Mudflap combed the industrial areas and had a nose for finding lost and/or abandoned gas tanks. He would trade them in at the gas plant for tank credits. He was persuasive at the plant, because they were always behind paying the bill. He was really building the business and becoming a good salesman.

For the home gas end, he did propane service too. Mudflap was swapping 100-pound tanks and servicing gas equipment with no formal training. Twelve hour days became regular business. Then the boss started having trouble keeping up paying Mudflap. The overtime was too expensive for the struggling business. He confided in Mudflap, told him his woes. Explained the illegal banking trick of kiting checks. Mudflap, still too naive to grasp the scope of this kind of business practice, fell for his crying and agreed to exchange his overtime for use of the truck on Saturday and was allowed to cut firewood off the back lot behind the store.

The truck was a good deal, and Mudflap made the most of it. The truck was an old, rotting 1970 Ford one ton. Like the whole business, it looked good on the surface, but the underneath was rotten. The cab mounts gone so bad that the clutch rod had to be extended to properly fit the transmission.

Just like at the gas plant, the owner was behind with his bill at the mechanic's. Mudflap used his persuasive salesmanship and nose for abandoned tanks to keep the mechanic happy too. He slipped him welding rods, supplies, and scrap steel; anything to keep that death trap of a truck going.

Mudflap had one day off a week. His girl and the motorcycle took precedent. They rode all over, with and without the gang. Gillette's Castle was always fun, and there was a house close by that they really liked and dreamed of buying. On the way back they rode up to Cobalt where Mudflap heard stories of land possibly left from his father's mess, and rights the family was supposed to have at the mines. They checked out the lake his father used to own. Finding out that the old family house at the far end was for sale, Mudflap talked to the owner. Since the boys were out of school, the parents talked about moving to a nicer house. Mudflap went back to tell his family about the old house. Somehow it all fell into place. It was a romantic gesture on the husband's part to buy back what the mom had lost. In hindsight it may not have been the best idea. Everyone was caught up in how beautiful the setting was: house by itself, private, at the end of the lake and Great Hill, the mountain directly behind, where you could hike up and see for miles.

Back at the gas company, Mudflap worked hard. The owner kept bouncing checks, and crying broke, even though Mudflap kept expanding the business, salvaging tanks, keeping the truck on the road, and holding up his end.

They were moving into the new house; it had

been a long day. The parents of Mudflap's girl insisted she be home, not trusting her to sleep over. Lord knows why? The ship they worried about had sailed a couple years ago. Mudflap had to drive her back because she was too tired. It was an ok ride to Durham. They used her car rather than one of Mudflap's junks. The cutest little Pinto you ever saw, white with a blue vinyl top. On the way back, the Flapster was getting tired. He rolled down the window, turned up the radio, bounced in his seat. He was on Route 66, just past the Dairy Queen, four miles to go, he thought. He closed his eyes for a second. WHAM! He was startled awake as he hit the guardrail right at the first post. It flipped and the opposite side of the car hit again, and the cute little Pinto was on its vinyl roof.

The dash board was flickering, the wipers came on. Mudflap freaked out. Thinking it was going to explode, he scrambled out the driver's window, glad that he had opened it. He stood back and looked at the mess in shock. Then he did one of the bravest/dumbest things of his life. He went back, crawled in and shut the car off. For some reason he didn't want to see it blow up.

Cars smell the same when you roll them over. The gear oil and gas, the broken glass, other fluids, the battery upside down, bent steel. It all merges together into one scent.

It didn't take long before a state trooper came along. It must have been past 3 a.m. Nobody else was out. Obviously shaken up, Madflap told the trooper he fell asleep. The trooper said, "You can't say that. It's against the law to fall asleep." "Really?" Mudflap replied. "Yes," the trooper said. Mudflap explained about the moving. The trooper told him, "It was foggy and you were unfamiliar with the road."

Lucky to be alive, and to have a trooper who was another great guy, Mudflap skipped the hospital this time and took the ride home. He thanked the trooper and went in to face the music.

Things just were not getting better at the gas company, although Mudflap had been sticking with it almost longer than all his other jobs put together.

The tree service his brother worked for fell apart from bad management and probably not taking care of their help.

Talk of starting a tree service got serious.

Mudflap confronted the boss at the gas company about the dangerous truck, and all his efforts for an unreasonably low pay. He said it was time for a raise, and the truck needed to be upgraded - basically an ultimatum with teeth. If he did not come up to speed, Mudflap was going to go cut trees.

The crying no longer worked; Mudflap walked out.

The Last Two Straws

Mudflap always felt as if there was a Guardian Angel watching his back. God looks after drunks and fools. Mudflap fit the bill in both spots, he thought: always quick with a sarcastic joke, or to poke fun at himself.

Mudflap looked to the future with enthusiastic energy, giving everything he could to the new tree service.

His brother had a bigger nest egg to jumpstart the service and the purchase of equipment. He was about to buy a big rack-body truck to haul brush. Mudflap stopped him, and told him about a chipper he saw for sale while on the road selling welding supplies. Mudflap was already sick of packing brush in little trucks, and saw a bigger leap forward with a chipper.

Mudflap's intuition was spot on. When they went to the farm where the chipper was, "Smiley", as they called him, had a nice little dump truck, too, that he wanted to sell. The perfect combination: a Ford 600, and a Vermeer 1600. A tough, almost indestructible pair that would end up servicing the brother well for years to come.

"Smiley" got his name from the grin plastered across his face that almost never left his countenance. Mudflap figured it was due to the vast farm, the beautiful house, and the boatload of money he obviously had.

The brother almost balked at the purchase, crying that it would take almost all his funds. Mudflap pointed out all the good features of the deal, and the fact that he was there to help him set up for free. The parents were not charging any rent. There was plenty of room at the lake house for the equipment. The brother was not really at any risk at all.

With guidance from little brother, big brother's income was about to take a quantum leap.

By now Mudflap was becoming a seasoned salesman. He was bringing in jobs.

He was now climbing, and using ropes, really growing into the job. His brother still did most of the big climbing tasks, having years more experience. Mudflap hustled as the ground man.

That nasty edge of a temper still hung in the air around his brother. Mudflap always had to be aware of it, and was used to managing his brother, being careful what he said, as his brother might take something out of context, and go off screaming. His brother did not like it if Mudflap stopped at all, not understanding that he sometimes was just taking in the situation. If Mudflap stopped, his brother would yell out to snap to it! Mudflap was used to working like a mad man, but they were no longer in the woods; they were doing residential tree work.

Mudflap still worked way too cheaply, but was now adding sales commissions to the bill. He could tell his brother hated to pay commissions to Mudflap.

Upon arriving on a Mudflap-sold job, his brother would take charge and take over sales from there, not paying Mudflap for any extras, and grabbing up the neighbors, too as they went. Mudflap let it go, but noticed he always sold cheap prices to ensure a sale. Mudflap realized that if he were to spend more time with the customer selling quality, he could get more. If he would just let Mudflap do his job, they both would make more. But you had to be careful what you said to big brother, and if you did speak up, you had better be far enough back from those long arms.

One day they were on a Mudflap-sold job, right across the street from Mudflap's girl's house, taking down a big sugar maple. Brother was in the tree, Mudflap cutting on the ground. Brother would cut a section off. Once it hit the ground, Mudflap would cut until brother reset his position ready to cut again: regular business.

Remember: Mudflap was to hop to it between cuts. A climber is supposed to wait for the ground man to finish, then proceed. Somewhere brother forgot protocol, or did he? We will never know.

Mudflap was bent over sawing away as fast as he could, but then something made him stand up for a second. Instantly, a large section of the tree took the skin off his nose, and knocked the saw out of his hands. His hat saved the skin on his forehead, but Mudflap was stunned, and stepped back in a daze.

Mudflap must have gone over to his girl's house for some relief, but doesn't really remember.

They did finish the job though, and he got to go home that night.

Mudflap let it go; it had to be an honest mistake.

Time passed.

Mudflap sold two big jobs in close proximity to each other. He suggested they bring an extra guy to help. A Grand Slam! They doubled the rate with half the cost. Mudflap felt great.

Big brother begrudgingly paid out the large commission due.

It all went so well that they kept the extra guy on and continued the new system.

Then things started to go the wrong way. First Mudflap had to listen to the crying about the cost of the extra guy on the payroll. His brother had been spoiled by the fact that you don't need workman's comp on family members. So to offset his expenses, brother would only pay the men to drive one way to the jobs. When the job was over, the money stopped, and he wore a watch. Then they stopped at the gas station on the way home and serviced the equipment. Mudflap had to unload the truck when they got home. Brother was afraid to leave the saws and climbing equipment in the truck overnight. Mudflap tried to maintain a good attitude. Even his mom saw what was happening, rolling her eyes as brother shouted orders to load up in the morning, while he was still in his underwear. This went on for a while.

Then the hired help (his brother's friend), ran his mouth because he wanted a raise, and let it slip he was already getting paid more than Mudflap. The betrayal was unforgivable. Brother's reason was that the friend had a house and a family. Mudflap said, "I will never have a house or a family at this rate."

Mudflap quit. When he's done, he's done.

Coincidentally, the gas company had been in touch wondering how Mudflap was doing, and wanted him back. Who wouldn't! Mudflap was the sucker of the century.

The gas company leased a newer Ford 250, and still had the old 350 for heavier loads and back up. The new truck was offered up as part of the deal. Mudflap returned and instantly got back into the groove.

It was 1978, Mudflap was now 20 years old. He had been saving money and really wanted his own house. Living home with brother was not as fuzzy as it was before, to say the least.

His mom had given her Pinto to Mudflap. But the insurance was high; he wanted to save more. Mudflap had a plan.

There was no required insurance for motorcycles at the time. Mudflap had the use of the new truck, but was not quite as trusting as he had been before. He wanted an ace in his pocket. His big 900 was worthless in the snow and ice, but in a pinch, he could drive a dirt bike in the winter. A small, 175 cc bike would be easy to handle, regardless of conditions, and his girl could handle it for some trail riding. He could ditch the insurance bill, and have a back-up vehicle. Get money for the car. It was a solid plan. His mom was mad because he was going to sell the car and told him not to. Mudflap knew what he was doing, but it made more tension in the house.

Mudflap was on his way home with the new little motorcycle hanging out the back of the hatchback Pinto, happy thinking of all the fun they were going to have with the brand new bike. All of a sudden, the muffler blew off the Pinto. It couldn't be louder. Combined with it dragging underneath the car, it was making too much noise to keep going. Mudflap had to pull over to remove it from under the car. Damn, he thought, got to put money into the car right before he was going to sell it.

He was on State Highway Route 17, approaching the top of a hill where there was a bit of a curve, not the best place to pull over. But the noise was just way too loud, even for Mudflap, who loved loud engines. As he started to pull into the breakdown lane, some lunatic in a big, dark car was flying up the road, at what must have been almost 100 miles an hour, passing the oncoming traffic. There was no room for Mudflap and no time to react. Had he not been pulling over already there was no question in his mind that he would have been hit head on. The wind from the bigger car shook the Pinto as it went by, Mudflap giving that last little jerk of the steering wheel to the side, shaving off the inches he needed to survive.

Once again, Mudflap found himself on the side of the road in shock. At least the car was on its wheels, and it was only a muffler problem. Mudflap, cool as a cookie at 100 miles an hour on his bike, or 60 ft. in the air cutting a tree top, was rattled by how close he had just come to getting wiped out.

He really started to believe he had an Angel watching his back.

He got under the car and ripped the muffler off, twisting and kicking it loose. He went home in a bit of a daze.

To this day, whenever Mudflap pulls out on a curve, especially on state highways, he always pulls over slowly leaving room for vehicles that he can't see: that crazy guy on a motorcycle, or lunatic in that car, giving them that little extra space to squeeze by, if they need to.

Back again at the gas company, Mudflap outdid himself again. His nose for free tanks turned to large, abandoned propane tanks. He started scoffing 500 and 1,000 gallon tanks from horrible spots, using the pipe crane with a boat trailer winch on the back of the one-ton truck. He used a come-along hand winch to assist the crane. He did super feats of daring all alone, managing not to shear any valves as he dragged the tanks out, trying as hard as he could not to blow himself up.

He got burned badly servicing a hot water heater. It took the skin off one hand, but he wrapped it up and kept going.

The bulk tanks he put in service were filled by their gas supplier. They did so well, the boss was able to legitimately buy some new bulk tanks.

The neighbor lady, who sported the football field, became the secretary. Poor old girl would be freezing at her desk in that block building, waiting to get paid all the time too. She and Mudflap shared a place under the bus.

Finally, Mudflap's biggest goal was reached: a house, and he was still only 20 years old.

Mudflap made his own deal (without a realtor) on a condemned house across the lake from his mom. He also did his own financing. He had paid off two loans on both new Kawasakis. His credit was good. He had a good down payment, everything well in place. But the bank started to balk. They wanted more. Long ago there was talk about another bridge to assist and or replace the Arrigoni Bridge. The father had in his land mass sections of a swamp in Portland thinking the state would buy him out someday.

As Mudflap grew up he heard stories and started to figure out how his farther got so much land back in the old days. An old-time farmer and logger, uncle on his mom's side, owned mountain ranges that he logged with oxen. As he aged he got rid of the land to ditch the property taxes. He lived until he was 96 years old, with his wife on a little farm with no electricity or indoor plumbing. Mudflap remembers them, because whenever his father came for one of his visits, they would always stop to see the uncle. The uncle's wife, a few years younger, would throw a pail on a rope into the hand-dug well for all their water. They cooked on the pot-belly stove, which was also the only source of heat in the house. The town left them alone, being the only ones left around living without modern sanitation. He had oxen way into his eighties, went to the country fairs with them, and was a real historic figure - a true New Englander. Mudflap has Polaroid snapshots of the uncle, himself and his brother on the porch of the old house. The uncle's opinion was that the problems at that time in the world were caused by "Electricity and the A-Tom Bomb."

The boys each had deeded sections of the swampland. It was like joke land, monopoly money. Mudflap told the banker he had some land to put up as collateral. The greedy banker liked that idea very much. The deed read northwest by this and that, deed stuff. Never once mentioned it was under water. The banker took the deal, hook line and sinker. Mudflap made use of the worthless land to leverage himself into his first real estate deal. Mudflap was peeking out from under the bus, seeing some light, and getting some fresh air.

The house was a little ranch, with a drive-under garage, perfect for his bikes and tools. But it was a mess, needing lots of work. It was condemned for numerous reasons. Fleas jumped you when you went in, and Mudflap had to set off a bug bomb to smoke out the house.

Tensions were high at home. Are you surprised?

Everybody wanted Mudflap out. It didn't matter if his place was condemned or not. Get out and camp in the house, that was their attitude.

Poor old stepdad, he finally got out of that crazy neighborhood to that nice, quiet spot on the lake. Mudflap was almost out. The dad was older than the mom and he had been popping nitro glycerin tablets for a couple of years. Mudflap, basically being thrown out, was scrambling to get his belongings organized. Big brother had control over the garage, so Mudflap was using the attic to store some stuff while he started to renovate his new house. The dad should have chilled out, but he jumped the gun, wanted all of Mudflap's stuff out. The guy, usually more calm than the rest of the family, threw a hissy-fit when Mudflap was going into the attic. Mom came to Mudflap's defense. The dad started stomping his foot in protest and increased the volume in his dialogue. Then, with a gasp, he clutched his chest and fell back in his arm chair. Mudflap watched as his pants went wet, his eyes glazed over, and he slumped to the side. He was gone, dead on the spot.

With all that was going on, the funeral was a blur. Mudflap had to get out as quickly as possible because brother was taking over fast, and mom didn't need more trouble. Mudflap also had a mortgage, a renovation, a lot at work was happening. He didn't have time to deal with his brother.

The owner of the gas company bought a big tank truck to service the large tanks Mudflap was acquiring and reinstalling. A driver was hired to drive the truck. Not a problem, Mudflap was too valuable doing all his other jobs, and he didn't want that job anyway.

The deal killer was, because of the industry standard, nobody was going to drive that truck cheaper than Mudflap was working for. The guy was older, that seemed to give him some kind of status, even though filling tanks was the easiest job in the shop.

The owner was always stretching everybody, constantly on the verge of bankruptcy. Even though Mudflap was the backbone of the whole shop, there was no extra money for him as the company moved forward.

It was ridiculous. Mudflap was doing five different jobs and was now moving down the ladder.

By this time, Mudflap knew a lot of people in the industry: customers, suppliers, and competition alike. A lot less naïve, and now becoming a lot more cynical, he was fed up, couldn't believe it was happening again. Build a guy's business, and you're the first one to get the shaft. Mudflap quit for good this time. When he's done, he's done!

With a mortgage over his head and paying utilities and all, unlike his brother at home living for free, stuffing all the money in his pockets, Mudflap was under the gun and had to act.

Mudflap flipped sides, in a vindictive and mean spirited sort of way, made a move to the competition of the gas company. Mudflap made a deal with a small, family-owned gas provider and welding supply company. His focus was to be welding supply; he disliked the propane end of the business. He was to do the service route and expand the customer base. He made it clear that he expected to be paid for the sales work, the expansion to be his way to move forward. He was expecting to earn his way; he didn't want handouts.

Mudflap left both businesses he worked so hard to establish. The idealistic idea of loyalty, gratitude and integrity, in that blind, innocent sort of way, would be forever lost for Mudflap.

At The Doorstep

Mudflap, now working at the other gas company, once again threw himself completely into his work.

Girlfriend was now fiancee, and she moved into the house, along with two new puppies. Toggle, the dog (who lived at mom's), was a regular visitor and well named for her back and forth visiting action.

Dogs always had a grounding effect on the family. Toggle came along as the boys got bigger. A black Lab mix, she kept Suzer going and caused trouble. Stealing steaks off neighborhood grills was a favorite trick of hers. You really had to watch her; one time she took a ham right off the dining room table. The old neighborhood was glad to see her go.

Old Suzer just would not die. She had cataracts, was deaf, she limped, had a little mange on her back. You would have to stomp on the floor to get her attention. Fell down the stairs a few times, but just kept going. She feared nothing - the bravest dog ever - except the veterinarian. It always freaked her out to go there, and she would shake uncontrollably. One day during the happy time, when the family was still enjoying the new lake house, it happened. While Mudflap was at work, the rest of the family conspired to put Suzer down. They knew Mudflap would never go along with it. They took her in, Suzer knowing all those years that it was the place that would get her. Mudflap was crushed. She was the first domino to fall. Then the tree service, and the stepdad dropped. The happy time was over.

The fiancee tried to make arrangements for the wedding. Her parents stalled, were not for it. The real world of work was not fun, because you had to pay bills. She was happier on the bike. Mudflap talked about being self-employed, but totally against it, she stated, "The self-employed people I know - fathers, brothers, uncles - worked all the time and didn't have the time for their wives and families."

Then Sanshaw, one of the puppies, got hit by a car, dead and gone. Fiancee joined a life support group, the EST Training. Toggle disappeared, never to be seen again. (Probably got shot for stealing - chickens or something, she was such a bad ass.) The support group supported ditching responsibility. Her dad lured her back home with a new car. Mudflap got traded for a new Camaro. He was left alone with Zeek the pup.

Zeek, another Lab mix, had short hair, the colors of a Doberman, but long floppy ears and a long tail.

Mudlap did well in the new job, but the employer kept stalling, reviewing his sales. His patience was thin, and tired of being taken advantage of, he was not going to let it go on very long. When Mudflap finally confronted his boss, he could see he was not going to get paid for his sales. It was another dead end. Mudflap was done.

He walked out, but not unprepared. He had been fixing up a truck. He built one out of two trucks, just like he did with the old Saabs. A one ton F-350, like the old gas company truck he started with. When he left the first gas company, he took the old-death trap with him. Telling that slippery con-man that nobody was dying for him in that truck; he was taking it to cut up and use for parts.

Mudflap fixed the rotten floors first, and worked up through the whole truck; it was ready and so was he. After helping so many small businesses, and having been exposed to his parents' small business, and garages and contractors, any hesitation or worry about his mortgage was gone, along with his girl.

Chapter 3

Self Employed

Up the Proverbial Ladder

Now finally, Mudflap was on the top of the ladder, and holding the bottom, and had to carry it from the middle. He was about to get some more hard learned lessons. When they say it's "lonely at the top," they really were not kidding.

Mudflap, now alone at the house, had a lot to do, as always. A house is a scary thing for a young person financially. Any big bill, like a well, furnace, or roof, can break you. Mudflap knew this and that is why he was self-employed. At his last job he only brought home a little over $250 a week. His girl could eat that much at lunches and dinners every month, easy. He worked five days a week at his job, did his own jobs on Saturdays, worked on the house evenings, leaving only Sunday, but with a house that got grabbed up too. He could make the same money doing tree work in one day as he did all week. The math was easy, ("take that, algebra") to get anywhere he had to quit.

His girl just didn't get it; self-employment was the way to her happiness, too. Mudflap was still in denial.

The old Eve and the apple thing again. Mudflap ahead of the curve, (on a totally different road), had intuitively proposed an idea to his girl before they bought the house. He saw all the work as a crap fest too. He, too, wanted to drive the bike all the time in the warm sun. She hated to be cold, hated winter. He had his father in Florida they could bounce off of. He said to her, "Let's ditch everything in Connecticut and go to Florida."

Oh no, that was a crazy idea. She would not go along with that at all. The EST Training group, dispensing the electric kool-aid, gave her the same idea Mudflap had. She always loved a song played to her. Her old boyfriend from Newington had connections, and for years before Durham, she had front-row seats at every concert that came to town. So, high on the kool-aid, with her new-found freedom, she grabbed the first long-haired guy with a guitar who came along, married him and took off to Florida.

Mudflap heard about the wedding. Her grandparents kept asking where was Mudflap? Wasn't he going to stop her? They were his only real allies in the family. She wanted "The Graduate Movie Moment", but no motorcycle roared up to stop the wedding. Mudflap was not going back to wait in line like she had them doing in school.

So off to Florida she went. Of course that marriage was short lived; that was satisfying for Mudflap to hear. But she stayed in Florida, the whole family and lots of her friends followed her. She's there to this day; Mudflap hopes she's warm.

It does get cold in New England. Mudflap went through a lot of trouble to put in a wood stove that tied into the heating system; it was very innovative.

Good thing he put antifreeze in it, he worked such long hours he couldn't keep up feeding the stove. During the warm weather, as he did tree removals, he started piling up wood to sell for the winter. He had a mountain of wood bigger than his house come winter, but too poor to burn it himself, he sold every stick.

That wood pile was the tip of a big iceberg. Mudflap was starting to stress out his neighbors, a fact that was escaping him at the time. Neighbors don't like contractors: they keep stuff, they do stuff, they make noise, they work late and early, too. Neighbors especially hate trucks and equipment. Mudflap was still naive about a lot of things.

His neighbor directly across the street was like the photo negative of Mudflap. He rented the house, had a regular job, a wife and children, and stayed out all night and partied while Mudflap went to bed early to get ready for the next day. The neighbor was a Harley guy; Mudflap rode a rice rocket. The neighbor had tons of friends. Mudflap had only a few close buddies.

The bike gang, which was hardly a gang at all, was basically just four guys with occasional extras tagging along. It consisted of Mudflap, the two friends from school, and a cousin of one of the friends who was the top mechanic. His dad was the group's role model, an old-world mechanic, a country-style living New Englander.

We will leave the escapades out; the short story is the gang slowly dissolved as the girlfriends couldn't agree on where they wanted to go, and everyone started looking in other directions. One member left for Florida, never to be seen again, completely unrelated to Mudflap's girl's exit.

The other school friend ended up in Florida too, but again for a completely different reason. He ditched his sweet, nice girl for a high-voltage crazy woman, who out-partied everyone, and dragged him into the world of dealing cocaine, guns and paranoia. Mudflap stayed clear; they were not minors anymore - it was serious business. They ended up getting busted, crazy woman did time. Mudflap had nothing to do with it. The last member, the mechanic, had a falling out with Mudflap over setting up the first big truck Mudflap put into service. To his credit, he was the only one in 40 years to ever say he was sorry about anything.

Mudflap is alone. His now-closest friend was a younger guy from back in Durham who worked after school helping the Con-man at the gas company. We will call him the K-man. He spent time under the bus hanging with Mudflap and the secretary too. The Con-man had a good group of loyal helpers; he let them all down. His business folded not long after he lost Mudflap.

The K-man, younger, was number three in the first crew Mudflap put together. Number two was another Durham boy from Mudflap's class of 1976. This would be the only three-man crew that would hold steady for any length of time. It was before Mudflap had more machines, the operation more primitive. The body off the old gas truck, heavy steel rack, with the pipe crane in the corner, lifted heavy logs. Later they would try an electric winch on it, but it failed. The old boat hand crank held up well, and was dependable. At least the logs could not blow up.

The work was hard and tempers would flare. Mudflap did all the climbing and cutting, anything dangerous was his job. Mudflap then, and always in the future, would take good care of his help. He knew all too well how it felt to be unappreciated. But you must hold your ground - human nature is to take advantage of situations.

Mudflap often thought of Aesop and his fables, (from the Rocky and Bullwinkle show), "familiarity breeds contempt." Oh so wise.

Number two's ego got in the way, putting a wedge between the men. He stormed off with the statement "all you do is cut the tree down, and we got to pick it up." He fancied himself an aerial photographer, had a license to fly, and rented planes. He crashed not long after, dead and gone.

K-man moved up to the number two spot. They did a lot of hard jobs cheaply, but made more than working for someone else. Years started to pass, their relationship was on and off again, other guys, other long days, and other stories, it all started to blend.

It was lonely at the top; sometimes he did not know which end of the ladder was up. Guys would quit, and Mudflap finished jobs alone. The help would not show in the morning; he would take his girlfriend to work. He learned to think out of the box and would crash whole trees in crazy tight spots because he had either inexperienced help, or a woman on the job. Being reckless, became regular business, "If it fits, it goes" was the saying.

He did try some other types of contract work, doing home improvements, but it was always the same. You got involved with these guys, their greed and egos, for every sub-contract job he did they would always find a way to short him. He found if he stuck to the trees, it was hard, but no materials, cut and dry deals, get paid and move on.

Mudflap, distracted, paid little attention to his brother, just went home to see his mom.   He purposely did not compete with his brother, and sold work further away from Portland. He worked his way up through Newington and into West Hartford, where he found more trees and houses together in any place than he had ever seen before.

While Mudflap was minding his own business, big brother was not satisfied just having a free place to live and run his business. He caught the mom at her weakest low point after losing her husband, and got the whole house signed over to him. Next he moved his girlfriend in and completely took over the house.

Feeling empowered, brother became more abusive than he had been for years. When questioned about what was going on, brother flew into a rage and started swinging. When Mudflap defended himself, brother's girlfriend jumped on his back. As Mudflap reached behind himself with both hands, trying to get her off, brother clocked him in the jaw with a full swing. Unable to block the punch, a chunk of tooth went flying. Mudflap was now fighting two of them; it was a mess!

Talk about from bad to worse, it took a couple weeks for them to calm down enough before Mudflap could go see his mom.

Mudflap got involved with a woman who came from an abusive relationship, a single mom with a young teenage boy. Here is where he needed a smack in the head, and there was nobody around to do it. As the help came and went, the girlfriend was still there. The longer she stayed, the farther up the ladder she went, till she really started having status.

Starting the business with a mortgage and a real overhead was a lot more complicated than starting out of a parent's garage. Banks don't cooperate with small businesses. They trash them, and hold them down, even though small businesses are a major part of the American economy. Mudflap didn't have the luxury of starting out with a bigger truck and chipper. He had to have a do-it-all vehicle, and work up from there. He put pipe staging in the racks on his truck, and would go down the road with a ten-foot pile of brush on back. It was a lot harder but the system worked great, and he did well. He needed to grow, but the bank didn't even want to talk to him.

He used the land trick again and bought a chipper. That helped. He second-mortgaged the house and bought a big truck. Now with his house on the line, he expanded the crew. Before he knew it, the crew smashed up the truck. Then they quit because they didn't want to help fix the truck.

Set him back months, but he bought another big truck.

Trouble was, he kept ending up on the reverse side of the ladder, always caring more about the guys working for him, and they never returned the gesture.

Mudflap was the boss but always at the bottom of the ladder. He kept going and growing, despite all obstacles.

As Mudflap started to become more of a seasoned veteran in the tree industry, he stumbled on an idea that was years ahead of his competition. He bought out a building-wrecking company. An old guy was retiring, and he had cranes. The whole tree removal industry was about to shift into bigger tree-eating chippers, more complex lift machines, and cranes were to be in the forefront of the big, more complex jobs.

Mudflap was spot on.

Chapter 4

The Proverbial Ladder Breaks

The Reversal

There comes a time in a man's life when he has to face up to the fact that he can't always make things right.

Sometimes the squeaky wheel does not get the grease - it gets replaced!

Words of Wisdom from Mudflap. Over and Out !

The once quiet, little lake road now is a busy place. Halfway down the street, towards the lake, is the working man on one side and the party man on the other. The working man, of course, is Mudflap, and the party man is everybody's buddy.

Expanding the operation, Mudflap did have a commercial lot to store most of the equipment he bought from the wrecking company. He did take many pieces of equipment home, too. His yard started to take on a scary appearance.

To treat himself to a toy he felt he deserved, he had bought earlier, a Harley Davidson 1982 full size FLH Sport. That year the Harley Company bought the motorcycles back from AMC. The AMC line of products had gone downhill. History has shown us, Harley did a good thing. Mudflap was on board, thought he was buying a real collectable.

Mudflap would take one of his bikes out to sell work regularly. The neighbor "Buddy" rode his a lot, too. Combined with Buddy's friends, and all the bikes being loud, the peace of the neighborhood was under attack. All the young men, oblivious of the abutting neighbors, carried on at all hours.

The neighbors, unable to do anything about the motorcycles, became more focused on Mudflap's equipment.

Big brother and his now wife-to-be were in complete control of the mom's house and of mom herself. She was traumatized from losing her husband and now her freedom. She left Connecticut and went to live in Maine with her sister.

The aunt, who had been there for the family all these years, retired from teaching. With her friend, she bought a marina, cottages, and a restaurant on Sebago Lake. Her later years were a party in full swing. The mom left Portland to escape the brother.

Mudflap, pushing forward with backbone, tree removals paying the way, prepared the operation for the big expansion.

The neighbors started to complain about Mudflap's equipment.

Mudflap's empathy was pushed back from years of the selfish whining and crying of everyone from bosses to help. He was now much more cynical.

He brought more stuff home just to rattle all the cages of the complainers.

The mom started to call Mudflap from Maine at night; she missed him.

As the expansion proceeded, Mudflap's right-hand man, and now full-time mechanic, helped the preparation.

The neighbors were becoming a big problem; they were not going to stop. Neither was Mudflap; as always he had a plan.

The vacant lots behind Mudflap's were part of the old land mass of his father's. The father lost the land to the contractor who fixed the dam on Great Hill Lake, which the father owned. The state hired the contractor to fix the dam after the father, in a covert operation, blew the dam up.

He did this act because, at the time he owned the lake, everyone around it enjoyed the lake at the father's expense. The father wanted everyone to help keep the lake clean and install beaches all around. They just wanted to use it, and give the maintenance bill to him.

The neighbors around the lake would not cooperate, so the father blew up the dam, making the lake into a swamp.

The state health department got involved. They hired the contractor to fix it, and gave the bill to the father.

The father told the state, "You hired them, you pay for it." Basically telling the state to shove it!

Oh, well! Now you see, things were not going well with the mom, and then their whole damn lives blew up too.

Mudflap had a lawyer working on buying the many building lots behind his house, and a deal was coming to a close soon.

The neighbors now pushed for an injunction against Mudflap, citing too much equipment in a residential zone.

Mudflap was putting his land deal together; and he was about to have equipment on a construction site.

Mudflap always liked the game of chess, and channeling the game, he made his moves.

The powers that be were churning, the air thick with anticipation, Mudflap loved the adrenaline, and was eager for the battle to come. He was not going to take crap from anybody. Mom called at nights, and was becoming increasingly unhappy with every call.

Everyday after the tree job, Mudflap would be eager to get back to see the progress of the mechanic. As part of the mass equipment purchase, he set up his guy with a mobile shop, paid him as a sub-contractor, giving the man a very generous deal. After the third time he surprised the guy, and caught him working on his stuff instead of doing what he was being paid to do, Mudflap started to feel that old twinge of pain he had felt from his brother and the con man.

The next day was the closing of the land deal. The neighbors at the same time were coming down with the full weight of the law on their side. The game was down to the wire.

He had a talk with his men, one at a time. They all had issues, everyone wanted something, everyone jockeying for position. Mudflap told it straight, everyone agreed, the deal was going down.

Mudflap slept well that night. In the morning, he went to the closing, the smell of victory in the air. He felt alive; nothing was going to stop him now.

At the closing the mood was good, smiles and humor, all was well. Mudflap reviewed the documents; everything in order as things were wrapping up. Mudflap asked to see the deeds again; he had a question in his mind. The lawyer had everything laid out, ready for Mudflap to sign. Deeds read funny. He thought about his swampland, reading more carefully. He didn't like the description. Some things seemed to be different from what he had researched. He thought about his father, rushing out, liquidating as fast as he could. He thought about his mom calling at night.

It was like a switch turned on, a toggle switch. It was all clear as could be, they were all screwing him, everybody, every single one of them was taking advantage of him. He looked up at the lawyer, and shook his head. "These deeds don't line up," Mudflap said. "Something's not right, I can't sign." Mudflap walked out. He was done.

When Mudflap's done, he's done. This time he was really done, with everybody and everything. He was going to sell his house, fire the help, sell everything, and go to Maine, buy an old farm somewhere and do a re-boot.

The plan was clear in his mind. He walked out with a lot to do, but it was a totally different set of chores.

He walked outside in the fresh air, a different person. He could no longer be straight with everybody. He had to be careful how he did this.

He left a thick layer of beat-up skin behind him. When you're in a snake pit, you just have to be a bigger snake.

Mudflap was turning around in a coil, getting ready to strike!

Throw Away that Ladder

There is a reason animals tuck their tails in when running away.

Keep it Tight

Mudflap, Over and Out !

Mudflap, now enlightened, is not kidding himself.   He knows he has a big mess to clean up, and doing it right is going to be important to the future of his next venture.

The idea was to buy a quaint old farm setting, up country where he could do what he wanted on his own land, and run his operation without the need for a commercial property. He would stop trying to manage crews, stay hands-on at every job, produce quality, and have minimal waste. Only allowing himself to grow within his own capabilities, he would keep relying on others to an absolute minimum - a philosophy that would carry him far into the next millenium.

Mudflap would like to call himself a minimalist, but that's a joke!

The short story:

First order of business was to fire the mechanic. That felt good. Then he canned the other guy too, and called up the old friend K-man and made him a golden deal where he got most all of the equipment. The big stuff, went to service their buddy at a salvage yard. K-man got parking, rental for equipment, and other perks at the salvage yard. Along with a complete set of tree service removal equipment, stump machines, the works. All financed into one easy payment of just $900 a month, and six weeks of work already sold. K-man was set up better than Mudflap's brother.

The big quote Mudflap always got from every guy was, "All you do is cut the tree down and I do all the work."

Coincidentally, the Crazy Man, a couple years back, moved to Maine. Deep down he was a woodsman and hated the factory. Fastest guy Mudflap had ever seen with a shot gun, could pick off a woodcock in tight forest before Mudflap ever saw it fly. Mudflap transported a couple dump trucks and trailers up to his property for storage till Mudflap found a place.

He filled a 40-foot trailer with all his bikes, small equipment and tools, sold his house and was gone before Christmas.

Mudflap, always taking good care of the people in his life, took along his girlfriend. But before they left, he married her, to protect her interest.

Chapter 5

The Great Maine Adventure

A Fresh Start

The old saying, "You can run, but you can't hide."

If you run and hide, don't take any of your problems with you!

Words of Wisdom from Mudflap, Over and Out !

Mudflap ran multiple loads of equipment and cargo to Maine, with some drama and maintenance along the way. The most memorable experience was losing the brakes on one of the dump trucks going to the Crazy Man's place in Farmington. Mudflap rode the emergency brake and down shifted for 100 miles.

The aunt's place, in East Sebago, was a lot further south than Farmington, but Mudflap was not yet sold on any location. He just wanted an old fixer-upper house with a barn, to get established in. The only other criteria for a new location being: not too close to neighbors.

The mom bought a cute little cottage on Sand Pond in Baldwin, a short drive from the aunt's complex of rental cottages, marina, and restaurant on the very big Sebago Lake. Sebago, being 20 miles long and 7 miles wide, was like an ocean to Mudflap, very impressive.

The mom had not yet moved into her new cottage, still staying with her sister. She was glad to see Mudflap, and offered up the cottage for him stay at until he could find a place of his own.

Mudflap, and now new wife, moved in and enjoyed the cottage as a honeymoon spot. Although the proverbial ladder of Mudflap's business had been thrown out, the wife had brought a little step-ladder of her own.

The fun task of picking out a new home was now top on the list of things to do. Funny how, but not in ha ha sorta way, variables happen that change peoples' lives. Sand Pond, serene, had a cloud hanging over it. An overbearing neighbor thought it appropriate to just walk into the cottage without knocking. He first did this when the mom came over to visit Mudflap one day. Seeing her car pull in, gave him in his mind, an open invitation to come over and join the party. When he walked right through the door, startling everyone, the mom gave Mudflap a look that displayed fear. Everyone was uneasy. Mudflap, taken aback, hesitated to confront the physically large and overzealous neighbor. Mudflap was not looking for a fight right off the bat, still a newcomer to the surroundings.

When the neighbor finally left, the mom confided in Mudflap, telling him she was afraid of the neighbor, and that's why she had not moved there, it was not the first time he walked right in.

This was now another variable thrown into the

mix as Mudflap considered where he was about to buy his next home.

The aunt's practical experience and knowledge of the area was not lost on Mudflap. She told everyone about a nice little antique farm setting, picture perfect, like a postcard, nearby in Naples, on the North Sebago town line. It was the first place they went to see.

It was very nice, only five miles from the aunt's, picture-perfect as described: a Cape with a saltbox addition, tucked into the south side of a hill with a detached barn slightly above, giving it a stately air. There were beautiful large rock walls coming off the sides of the house and barn, surrounding the rest of the entire property.

The girls loved it; Mudflap was not so sure. First, the price was way out of his range to buy without a mortgage. Second was the hill, although giving the buildings a stately appearance, it was not the best layout for his trucks and equipment.

The stepdad, in his own wisdom, had left the mom with a trust fund that gave her a good monthly allowance, but with no access to any large chunk to spend. He had confided to the mom, without explaining it in detail, that despite Mudflap's mischievous escapades, he was not really going to be a problem for her in the future, and it was the brother who she should watch out for.

Mudflap wanted a property free and clear of

what he already saw as the greedy banking system. He was willing to camp out in a wreck of a house that had potential and was more suited for his equipment.

Ah, but the girls pushed their ideas. It was close to the aunt and all the fun at the lake and restaurant. Owned by a New Yorker who had already renovated it, the house was in move-in condition. It was easier for the wife, who wouldn't have to camp and renovate, and plenty of room for the mom.

Mudflap had a down payment, the mom had the monthly money.

At this point Mudflap was unestablished in the area as a contractor, and even though it was tempting, wanted to balk. But the girls'happiness was his most major concern. So with uneasiness in the back of his mind, but the well-being of his women a priority, he went along with the deal.

The upside of the arrangement was the extra cash in his pocket, because he only had to do a down payment. He was able to finance a new chipper and stump machine. All he had to do now was fix up the two old dump trucks, and he was in business again. Only now he was in debt again, too.

It was the beginning of the "happy time."

Choose a Direction

On the road of life there are no traffic signs; it's all about the landmarks.

Mudflap, Over and Out !

Mudflap closed the deal on the farm, got right to work on his trucks, making progress quickly. Dealing well with his first Maine winter, he was up for tasks at hand, enjoying the challenges of acclimating into his new environment. He was very aware that his funds were running out fast, and he had to get back to work soon.

Good old country boy that he was, he found joy and humor in the local color of the inhabitants. His farm in Naples directly abutted the town line, so he had a Sebago phone exchange. It was a toll call for him to call his own town hall. What a different world we live in; now he can call California at no extra charge.

He did have a neighbor just barely in sight of his house. They were old time Maine folk who had lived on the road for generations. At first they were very friendly, Mudflap a skeptical Connecticut person is always friendly, but aloof.

Connecticut gets a bad rap for being unfriendly. We are very friendly once you get to know us, but we're not in-your-face happy like a clown. We are skeptical of over-friendly people, who most always in the end want something. If we don't like something, we will speak up; you know where you stand. We try to be nice, but we don't want you in our kitchen at night. In a pinch, you can count on us to rescue you. Otherwise, wave, say hi and keep going.

Still shell-shocked from the last neighborhood, but enjoying the locals, he did wonder about the odd sign next door. It read: No Trespassing Spikes in Place. Interesting, Mudflap thought.

The neighbors would never end up complaining about Mudflap's trucks and equipment. But before he was done there, they would end up shooting two of his dogs for running deer. Fact is they just wanted easy hunting. Not wanting to go far into the woods, they'd rather plunk them out the back door. Their daughter, tough, Mudflap's age, would later walk down the road like she was headed for the OK Corral, with a large sidearm bulging out from under her clothes.

Spring came fast, Mudflap hurried to finish up his trucks. He started doing jobs around the area, feeling out the market.

Everyone was happy settling into the new property. They did have two dogs that came along from Connecticut. More Lab mixes, Sergeant and Spook, they were a fun pair. Sergeant got his name from guard duty, back in the equipment wars.

It was now 1986. A couple years earlier, Mudflap lost his buddy Zeek, who helped him through some tough times. He used to come to work with him. One day Zeek was left home because the job was on a real busy road, he got out and fell through the ice. The dog warden brought him back like a board in the back of his truck.

Mudflap liked the locals, didn't mind working cheaper for them; they worked hard too. He felt the New Englander bond. Not everyone was completely receptive to Mudflap. He found a label some gave him offensive, a new term he had never heard before: "Flatlander." Strange, he thought, the mountains around didn't seem any bigger than the ones back home. But it did remind him of something else: "prejudice," like he felt in Virginia. He began to understand what it felt like to be black.

Our African-American citizens have fought in every one of our wars, including the Revolution. They have earned their place in America. They deserve our respect and gratitude for the sacrifices they have made, and continue to make. No other minority we see in videos today get shot in the back as they helplessly run away.

As jobs progressed in the area, and summer lake people arrived, a letter came in the mail from one of Mudflap's favorite customers back in Connecticut. The letter read something to the effect: "What are you doing in Maine? I need you to come back and cut my trees." Then, when doing what Mudflap thought was a stupid, low cost job, just trying to build up friends and connections, a simple gesture would change his life forever. As the new customer reached out with the check, and just as Mudflap reached to receive it, his index finger and thumb squeezed back, the gesture clearly indicating he did not want to give him the check. He was not a regular, poor, hard-working Mainer. He was a hot shot with a nice piece of property. At the instant he did that rude little move, Mudflap, thought about his client back in Connecticut who wanted him to come back. Just like at the failed closing, a switch turned on. He knew he could easily make plenty of money to be in both states. Instead of running all over Maine, he could make one drive to one town: West Hartford. His plan was not to run all over Connecticut either, as he had before.

Finally he had focus on exactly what to do. Service the one town, and retreat to Maine for maintenance, projects, and R+R breaks.

Connecticut, the state that people from away call cold, and even rude, is a very accepting place. No matter what nationality you are, if you are willing to work hard at whatever you do, Connecticut welcomes you. If you are lazy, and want to take advantage of the state and its people, and just cry about how expensive it is to be here, then go. Connecticut doesn't need you and doesn't want to hear the whining.

The Yankee Boy / Flatlander was going home.

Back and Forth

When Returning from Battle be Sure to Keep Your Tail Held High

And Wag it Even if it Hurts

Mudflap, Over and Out !

Ahead of the curve as usual, Mudflap got back to Connecticut just in time as the K-man, already on fire, was on his way down crashing and burning. He found out the hard way that it was more than just cut a tree down and get all the money. He failed, even with all his perks at the salvage yard that Mudflap never had.

Mudflap kept a grueling schedule: five days working, four nights at a cheap motel, and back to Maine for the weekend. He was approaching 28 years old, and could keep the pace. Alcohol had slipped back into his life after his girl left, and he was burning the candle at both ends.

By the fall, he was ready to purchase a house in Connecticut, and wanted to be in before winter. The motel thing was getting old. He had commercial parking for the equipment and a contract on a perfect house with garages. He put the whole deal together, everything looked good.

The bank balked at the last minute, didn't like his assets with his wife and mom unavailable. A good down payment was not enough, or his other swamp deed in Portland. They wanted to attach the Maine house too.

Every small business person who ever tries to push ahead will tell you stories about banks. Small businesses are a huge part of our economy, and the banks brutalize them every chance they get.

Back in Maine, while Mudflap kept the pace working the tree service, the girls, with too much time on their hands, start to squabble, and the neighbors shoot the dogs.

Mudflap is going back and forth, trying to keep the girls happy. The bad news of the house falling through does not help morale, especially for the wife. The work schedule turns into ten days on, four off, saving travel. But it stresses out relationships all around. Mudflap brings home a lap dog for mom, a scruffy, little white thing named Champ.

Mudflap goes to the bank one day and sees his banker in the parking lot, driving an orange car kinda thing, so small it doesn't even have a name. He was in shock. This guy, playing god with his financing, couldn't even afford a decent car.

Knowing now it's going to take more time to get into a property, Mudflap rents half a duplex, and gets two garage bays. That place was a good deal, for the next year he would run a tight ship and make money out of that spot.

Mudflap's stepson, now sixteen, hates school in Maine and wants to quit and work the tree service. Help was coming and going, so Mudflap was all for it.

The happy time had been gone for a while. Mudflap was catering to all three of them.

The mom and wife really were not getting along now. While Mudflap and stepson are in Connecticut working, a blowout happens, mom leaves Maine. She goes to Florida for a wild sailors-style party, visiting the old girlfriend, trying to get her back. It was a fool's errand, all she did was go through all the money she could get her hands on.

Big brother, in the mean time, had sold the lake house and built himself a new home still close to the lake. He bought a waterfall that was land-locked on purpose by the father, because everyone thought it was too dangerous to build near.

Back at Mudflap's rental, the neighbor on the other side of the duplex, who didn't like Mudflap working odd hours, started complaining.

Back at the farm, the wife was alone with Champ. The story was, he got hit by a car, and she had to shoot him to put him out of his misery. Mudflap didn't buy it.

Being pressured to move out of his rental, Mudflap moved into a commercial garage and lived with his equipment.

His next dog, a Lab, would be the last he would ever have. She was run over by the carelessness of his stepson, while showing off, still only a puppy.

Tired and beat up, Mudflap is done with the stepson and his many careless acts.

Big brother is forced to take the mom in because he had sold her house.

It's the end of 1987. Mudflap is tired of everybody. He is exhausted even recalling it.

Something's Got to Give

If you throw enough mud against a wall, something's got to stick.

And when you're talking mud, you're talking to the right guy.

The Flapster, Over and Out !

It's late fall 1987. Mudflap, now living in a commercial building, has built himself a little apartment, making a second floor in the corner of the large block building. One huge garage door he can pull anything in through, and an entrance door, no windows at all. Mudflap knocked a couple of holes through the block wall to install some small windows. He was practically living in a cave.

Christmas had never been the same since he lost his girl. A cold settled in, the block building was freezing. When his work days were done, he didn't go out for any fun at all. He started to hide in his bed and just slept every chance he got.

Wife came and went to Maine, couldn't blame her for not liking the building. Mudflap got home when he could. He was catering to his wife and her son; felt it was him vs. them. He felt cornered, almost trapped. Mudflap had evolved. He had experiences a 29-year-old usually does not get, but he was still a primitive. Rough around the edges, drinking hard, he had developed a taste for scotch. Sarcastic by nature, he still liked to poke fun at any who dared spar with him. Add a half pint of scotch to the sarcasm, and he was damn mean. He didn't have a lot to be happy about. Channeling his British side, he kept his chin up.

Christmas came, wife made a statement that stuck with Mudflap. "You always get this way around Christmas." Yes, he thought, I do. Funny how Mudflap puts up with a lot, and a lot more, then the littlest comment or gesture causes the switch to flip, and he takes a totally different turn. Anyone who really knows Mudflap will attest to the fact. When people thought, or think today, they have Mudflap where they want him, he will zig when they zag, and "poof" he's gone.

The holidays passed, Mudflap went back to the block building. The weather turned against him, working outside or even on the equipment in the building became unbearable. He got in his bed and hibernated.

As he slept, the winds of change swirled, Mudflap oblivious in his sleep.

The wife kept the books. Mudflap, maybe not liking her at this point, still trusted her, never once looking into what she was doing.

Later he would find out she started to cut herself checks.

It was now 1988. The real-estate market was booming. The aunt had been right about the house being a good deal. In the spring market of 1986, Mudflap already saw an increase in the value of the farm. The fact that the property had been steadily increasing kept him going all this time.

Wife, being business partner and bookkeeper, was looking closer at the numbers than Mudflap. She told him now was the time to buy another property; there was plenty of equity.

The greedy banks had been having a field day with increasing values across the boards. Banks now competed with mortgage companies. Greed was in vogue, and they were processing loans at an unprecedented rate of speed. Wife told Mudflap to start shopping.

Now Mudflap had a mission he could work on, without cutting trees in the snow. He came out of hibernation.

His criteria: stay west of the river, and off the interstates with his trucks, and be as close as he could to West Hartford. Newington was too crowded with too many neighbors. So he looked in a new direction he had never gone before, directly west. Avon, prices as bad as West Hartford, Canton still high. As he went further west, the land became more rural. He felt it, as he came into cute little New Hartford, first town in Litchfield County, he was home.

New Hartford is full of steep hills, not the best for his trucks in the snow and ice. He always loved the Main Street houses in Durham. He found a big, old, in-town house, with a detached three car garage. Bingo! Private with hedges, he still had his parking for the big trucks near West Hartford. The house was right on the state highway, Route 44. He couldn't get lost, not knowing anything about the area.

This was to become the place where his life would stabilize and be his home.

Mudflap was not out of trouble yet; he still had some hurdles to go.

It was time for his Guardian Angel to give him a little nudge.

The deal was approved, and the closing on schedule. Mudflap needed to keep making money, work was slow in the winter. His new home, becoming close, was constantly in the back of his mind.

He was out selling work, a regular Sunday activity. He was going by a property he had quoted years back, saw a lady out in the driveway. Always catching someone outside was a plus, rather than knocking on the door. A very seasoned salesman, he had his techniques down, was looking for tree work, but found so much more.

Mudflap pulled in, got out, and introduced himself, bouncing off the fact that he had talked to her husband about the huge tree by the house. She informed him the husband was not going to hire him, he had left, and was gone.

As they talked, Mudflap looked into her eyes. She told him that she had six kids too, and gave a laugh, but her eyes were not laughing. Mudflap's pain from his whole sordid past absorbed her pain like a sponge. He was instantly in love.

The switch flipped and Mudflap's mission was clear.

It didn't matter if he was going to be with the lady or not. He was not letting the wife and her careless son move into the new house. If he had a chance for a new home in a new town, he was not taking them with him at any cost.

Chapter 6

A New Town, A New Life

Pay Back

They say, "If it's too good to be true, it's probably not."

Enjoy it while you can!

Mudflap, Over and Out !

Mudflap, after all he's been through, could still be idealistic; cynicism had not overtaken him completely.

He goes back to Maine and confronts his wife about wanting to move to New Hartford alone. She had been on the rollercoaster long enough too. Being friends for four years now, they were good at handling changing situations. They agreed to a fair settlement and scheduled the paperwork.

Mudflap, as you now know, doesn't like the greedy college system, the banks, nosey neighbors, and social injustice. High on his list of people who also need a good trashing are the worst of the worst, "Blood-Sucking Divorce Lawyers." Lawyers in general, Mudflap likes very much. They are always practical, mostly level-headed and in general all around good people to deal with.

But divorce lawyers are a completely different breed. When questioning a lawyer if they do divorces, they are very quick to say, "No, I do not," distancing themselves from such a despicable group.

Poor Mudflap really got some road rash this time. He foolishly went in thinking everyone was going to be fair.

The first hint that he was in trouble was when the wife moved back to Connecticut, and took all the bookwork with her. She forwarded all the mail, Mudflap's included, to her new secret address. The post office unbelievably refused to tell him where his own mail went. If he had had time to spare, Mudflap would have gone after the Post Master's job. Mudflap was becoming increasingly more overwhelmed with everything.

The schedule, coming fast, was divorce in the morning, house closing in the afternoon.   Mudflap was about to get flanked.

Mudflap's lawyer, from his friend's hotshot firm on top of City Place, (the biggest skyscraper in Hartford), was recommended as a good guy. Is there such a thing as a good rattlesnake?

At first Mudflap thought the lawyer was just trying to relieve tension in the situation by asking Mudflap tree questions.   He was more interested in Mudflap's advice than the job he was being being paid for.

There was a cloak and dagger thing, where he had the wife and the opposing lawyer in the next room, and he kept going back and forth to Mudflap.

He even complained, "I need sneakers for this."

The Bottom Line: The agreement Mudflap and wife had was gone. Mudflap's lawyer was not on Mudflap's side at all, not one bit. He said to Mudflap, "Oh no, that's not enough, you have to give her a lot more."

Mudflap didn't realize until it was too late, but now he got it.

The banks at the time had been processing those loans like a shop-size vacuum cleaner. The more they lent, the more they made, simple. The lawyers were drooling! There was extra money in the closing for Mudflap to renovate his new house. There was just too much money for Mudflap. Even though the interest was extremely high, it didn't matter to the lawyers. They wanted it, as much as they could get.

The two lawyers and wife with the stolen books extorted Mudflap for $150,000 because of a bridge loan. Even though the property was not sold yet, they were cashing it out. If he didn't sign, he didn't get his house, scheduled to close in two hours.

It would have been more honest to put a gun against his head and just plain rob him.

At that point Mudflap would have paid anything to get away from the nightmare he had been living for years.

Mudflap moved into his new home that night

for the first time, March 15th, 1988. The Ides of March, poetically perfect, the same day Caesar was stabbed in the back.

It's a great place to leave the chapter, but to give you a hint, the blood was just beginning to flow.

The Happy Time

"The Happy Time" was also a time when the German U-Boats ruled the seas.

We all know what happened to them!

Mudflap, Over and Out !

Mudflap, mad at himself for being so naive, mad at the bloodsuckers, and his back-stabbing partner, had an hour or so before the closing of the real estate. He was confident it would go smoothly; he knew the lawyers wanted their money.

He went for a walk down the street and wandered into the Civic Center shops. He spotted a liquor store, and thought to himself, I could go for a drink. He went up to the top of a parking garage, and looking out over the city, he drank most of a pint of scotch. He dropped the bottle off, and watched it break in the alley below. There was just enough left in the bottle for the friend he didn't have to share it with.

The poor paralegal, nice girl, had to deal with him at the closing. Elated to be free, he went to his new home. He did have an occasional drink before dinner for a few weeks or so, but now alone, with everything to do on his plate, he stopped drinking.

The happy time was here again. Just like at the new lake house, and at the new farm. And now he had a new girlfriend too - the lady with the six kids.

He started taking her to Maine, and they were having a very nice time at the farm. Later in the summer, he took her up country touring to Acadia, and places he never took the time to go to before.

The farm was on the market, the time was ticking, he would not own it much longer. The market was strong, or was it?

The reality, 1987 was the top end of the real estate bubble. The bridge loan was just an in-between loan. It was never supposed to be permanent. Now these days you could never get one without a contract for a sale. But the greedy mortgage system sucked Mudflap's loan through the tailwind of the boom. Mudflap remembers the loan officer saying it was a bit slow because of winter, and they could process the loan quickly.

What was really happening was it hit the top. The spring got off to a slow start, and the market went flat. Seasoned professionals saw it, the rest were in denial. The whole market hesitated; it was holding its breath.

Mudflap was too happy to pay attention to the market. He wasn't really studying it before, he blindly cut trees and kept working, only listening to what was on the news.

There he was in Acadia, sitting in a hotel room in Bar Harbor, waiting for his lady to finish in the bath. Thinking the farm was as good as gone, he thumbed through a real estate book. He put it down, disgusted with the cost of Bar Harbor prices. She was taking a long time. (Gee, never seen a woman do that before.) He picked the book up again. In the back was a little drawing of a house on a rock in the water for $45,000. It wasn't even a photo. Joking as his friend finally appeared, he said, "Hey, here is something we can afford." So for fun, they thought they would take a ride inland to Lake Sebec, in the Moosehead Lake Region.

It was a fun time. They got a boat ride. The place was so small, Mudflap thought to himself, this place would be a piece of cake to take care of. One of the reasons Mudflap is Mudflap, is that he has an imagination, and it gets him in trouble. He was embarking on one of the biggest projects of his lifetime, looking through a romantic vision. That vision would happen, but would take the next 30 years of his life and beyond to complete.

He took $5,000 of his renovation money for his new house, thinking the farm would soon be gone. He got owner financing for the balance. Happy to still have a place in Maine to go, he went on his merry way.

The six months that followed his purchase for the house in New Hartford were the happiest time he had had in a decade. For Mudflap, it was the longest, straight-stretch of uninterrupted happiness in his entire life, up to that point.

Reality Check

When you fly higher than you ever dreamed you could, be sure it's a clear day; the clouds can block everything you see!

Mudflap, Over and Out !

Winter was on its way, 1988 was wrapping up fast. The doom and gloom of the downward spiral of the real estate was now on all the news channels. Mudflap was getting pressure from the bridge loan company. The six month period they expected to be paid in was up, and they wanted a payoff.

The debts were ballooning. The farm sale was supposed to pay off the balance on money due the ex-wife. She had gotten only a deposit of sorts, because the lawyers got such big cuts. The ex-wife became a mortgage.

He had the bridge loan, the first mortgage on New Hartford, the farm loan left by mom, and the little island made five mortgages. He also had a lease on his pick-up truck and a tractor loan, making it seven loans altogether.

Luckily for Mudflap, he was not the only one in trouble, everywhere the talk of recession filled the media. They all had to work with him; everybody was in over their heads. It got so bad that the next year CBT, an old Connecticut bank, went bust, too, along with the Colonial Real Estate collapse.

Mudflap got caught up in the biggest recession to hit the Northeast since the Great Depression.

The relationship with his lady friend lasted two years. The first six months were Heaven, followed by eighteen months of Hell. He is still very fond of her today.

Although technically he was in default with the bridge loan company and his ex-wife, they both got paid regularly until satisfied. All others stayed on schedule until completion of responsibility.

It took Mudflap years to paddle out of that mess. The farm, which was still going to be a big part of his life for a long while, finally sold 20 years after the happy days of being there with his mom.

The divorce lawyer continued to bill Mudflap for a balance, and he made a couple of small payments. The bill kept coming with interest getting larger each time. Finally he called the billing department. He questioned the girl, asking where was the retainer, the money he paid up front? Her reply was what retainer? Turns out, they were trying to double bill him.

Mudflap pointed out that using the mail to double bill was a federal offense. He never heard from them again.

Chapter 7

Things Level Out

Flatlander

You get a lot better gas mileage when the road has less hills.

A nice level playing field makes for a more fair game too!

Mudflap, Over and Out !

The 1990s were here. With the recession in full swing, there is little hope of Mudflap selling the farm at all. He's not bothered by the flatlander attitude, and no longer pushes work in the area. He is more interested in just working on his real estate projects, and enjoying the environment.

He works all the time, with a half million dollar debt monster cracking the whip behind him. As long as he keeps paying something, the bank and ex-wife can't do anything to hurt him. Neither one is very happy getting strung along. That part makes Mudflap happy, and he got even more satisfaction from the fact they would never have loaned him that much money if he had asked for it.

Mudflap liked to work and liked a good joke; he kept working, and chuckling, enjoying their despair.

He met a real nice girl, a sweet little thing, a harmless, introverted bookworm, brought up by

Quakers. A girl who, had he met earlier in his more primitive state, would not have had anything to do with him.

Karma had turned things in a different direction. Still, things were far from easy; the tree service was no picnic. Mudflap was battled-hardened physically, emotionally, and financially.

His ability to cope with it all alone, made him ready, and worthy of taking on the most important of all tasks: a family of his own.

Back in Portland, big brother had already started a family, and begrudgingly had the mom in a little shack of a house next door. His complaints of his costs fell on Mudflap's deaf ears. Karma had taken a bite out of everyone's back end, nobody escaped.

Mudflap's old girl had come back a while before to visit the mom, and to feel out Mudflap. She had already been through one divorce, and was on a rocky road with the current marriage. Mudflap was not surprised, and not really interested; he was glad he dodged that bullet too.

The little island up country was still kind of a fantasy. He would go up, check on it, do a few chores, and dream of things he wanted to do to the property.

Main Street, New Hartford was the smartest move Mudflap had ever made. The in-town location hardly ever lost power and if it did, it was only for a short time. Mudflap could jump out onto the state highway, instantly responding to storms, saving his clients from tree disasters, and tending to regular nuisance tree problems.

Mudflap and his new girl are very happy, but not in that unstable, euphoric, infatuated, happy time kind of way.

Three decades had passed since he was a little boy playing in the field of dandelions between the highways.

His up and down life was finally on the level.

Family Time

Time for family, and, or, the people who mean the most to you, has to come first.

Squander that, and you Squander your life!

Mudflap, Over and Out !

April 22nd 1992, a baby boy was born to Mudflap and his Love. They are proud parents. The new mother left her job as an office manager.

Family coming first, she had no intention of returning. Mudflap had no intention of ever leaving his children alone, unattended, or brought up by anyone other than their mother.

The mother acclimated into motherhood and little New Hartford's social climate. She would become a volunteer for local organizations, as well as do things for the children. Later on she would become the treasurer for the Land Trust.

January 14th 1995, a baby girl was born to Mudflap and his Love. Now in the full swing of parenthood, the couple move into the second half of the decade; mother established in her role, and Mudflap making progress beating up the debt monster.

Maine became the family's favorite time together. Mudflap worked the buildings and the land, refining the farm.

Going up country was special; it took more

time to organize. They had a modest little boat and named it after the little island, calling it Phoebe Too.

Going to Phoebe Island was exciting. They would camp out in the house with a tent, because the house was so old, and a bit on the grubby side, to say the least. Mudflap, who got dirty and worked hard, was not up for sleeping in the dirt, too. He was becoming a bit fussy as time went on, and he liked clean living.

Mudflap had beaten the debt monster down to a less scary size. He targeted the bridge loan first, knocked off the private loan for Phoebe, and was rid of the ex-wife's loan too.

The real estate was coming back, and lake houses were taking a big jump. Seeing the swing and feeling frisky, Mudflap bought another island in the same town as the farm, Naples. He leveraged his farm's equity and it got him in the door.

The island named Pine seduced him. He started losing interest working on the farmland. Upon arriving in Maine, he couldn't get in his little boat and out of the barn fast enough. Out to the island they would go. He was connecting the family to the environment and the greater powers that be.

Mudflap's best friend was from the days back in the old neighborhood. They had stayed in touch all this time, well-bonded for one simple fact. They never wanted anything out of each other but friendship.

Aesop the philosopher's statement that "familiarity breeds contempt" again describes why all the other friends were gone. They always used their friendships to get something or a job. They wouldn't want to do the work, or they would ask for things that in any other situation they would never dare.

Always taking advantage of Mudflap, always wanting something.

Lots of people take advantage of friendships. The "over-friendly" type people that Connecticut is wary of.

The workers that don't last often start overly enthusiastic, channeling "The happy time." Then when they don't get instant gratification they quickly lose interest. These people, looking for trade positions, have no sense what it takes to actually be an apprentice in a trade. The Japanese gardeners understood it took years to develop skills and technique - not weeks or even a couple months.

We should install a proper guidance system in schools with a more refined emphasis on social behavior, and a more talent and/or interest based view of their careers. It would give the system and the people in it more stable, long-term results.

Mudflap's friend was a single dad, had two girls. They came to the Farm and Pine Island for campouts. Everyone was happy just to be together, pitch in and have some fun.

The New Millennium was approaching fast. Mudflap was as ready as he could be, ready as any of us could be, as we all entered the new social, economic, and political times to come.

With a stable wife and at least one stable friend, Mudflap pushed forward.

Chapter 8

The Year 2000

Times Change

Time is unstoppable; some things you try to move along, others you try to slow down.

Knowing what's worth attempting to influence is the key.

Mudflap, Over and Out !

Everyone across the world anticipated the year with excitement, and some feared a crash of the banking system and the internet. Midnight came and went, and as Mudflap predicted, nothing happened.

But a lot was going to happen, and fast, a lot faster than all of us were expecting or wanted. The nation and the world were changing, and so was Mudflap's own little world.

The year had just started. Mudflap's best friend, who was a single dad, was left with two girls after their mom short circuited, her "happy time" over. He was a great dad. One day his younger daughter came home from school, and the door was obstructed by something. Her dad was dead on the floor, coat on, keys in his hand - didn't make it to work. Died of a massive heart attack – Bang! Finished business. Mudflap was a pall bearer.

Hell of a way to start the new millennium.

Everyone was rattled, but the rest of the year was unmemorable, thank God.

Up country was starting to take a quantum leap from old Phoebe to new Phoebe. The little island turns into a peninsula when the lake is drawn down in fall. Walking out to check the island was an annual event. Mudflap bought a right of way to shore, and with the deal he got 22 acres for parking and to start a land base.

The neighbor, who he bought the right-of-way from, was a local businessman. He started his business life with a tree service, and after that, had his hands in all sorts of things. They hit it off well, and he was a great neighbor. He helped Mudflap connect with contractors. Using the farm again as leverage, old Phoebe became new Phoebe. The little island house was not grubby anymore. It was beautiful.

As part of the sales pitch, Mudflap's neighbor showed him a spot on the land that he thought was a good site to dig a pond. He hooked up Mudflap with a land-clearing operation and an excavator. The logs and pulp paid for the pond, and Mudflap's wildlife sanctuary was born.

When Mudflap was a boy, he'd built a reptile and amphibian pit in his back yard with mostly turtles - snakes got out too easily. Snakes were kept in aquariums in the house, escapees always causing havoc.

Mudflap reversed the idea, built the pond, and

all his friends moved right in. Frogs were in the pond
before the grass started to grow. Now the family had
a perfect lake house and the sanctuary for wildlife
walks too. Without the equity in the farm, and
servicing the debts, none of it would have happened.

The biggest financial disaster of Mudflap's life
over time blossomed into a beautiful new world, of not
only reptiles and amphibians, but mammals and birds
alike. Even a little herd of deer hang out by the pond
and wetlands.

A little more than a year after Mudflap lost his
friend, he lost his mom too.

His brother, more estranged than ever, buried
her ashes next to her husband, not inviting or even
telling Mudflap until after the ceremony was over. He
gave Mudflap a 35mm film container filled with some
of her ashes, and said, "Here, have your own
ceremony."

That summer Mudflap, wife and the children
had a candle-lit ceremony on the Phoebe Island
assisted by the moon. They sprinkled little bits of
Gram lightly through the blueberries, all around the
island. The next day Gram got a rough little stone
obelisk, facing outward, taking in the lake. Mudflap
can see it from his chair on the front stoop as he
watches eagles, hummingbirds and much more.

The First Decade

The faster time goes, the more you should slow down.

Unless you're working, then it's the opposite!

Mudflap, Over and Out !

The summer is over, and Mudflap is back to work. He drives in like any other day. He's sporting an old 1970 Ford. It's the same year as the old gas truck and his first tree truck, but a utility box type. He likes antiques, but doesn't have the time for the cute car style. His idea of antique vehicles is: easy to work on, cheap taxes and insurance; they pay their way. It had no heat and no radio, frills he doesn't bother with. By the time the truck leaves service, it will work for him eighteen years.

He rumbles up to the job. His help, waiting there, jumps out of his truck and hurries over to Mudflap, excitedly exclaiming, "New York is under attack!" As Mudflap gets out, his client, a nice old fellow, is at the door. Mudflap asked him, "You watching TV this morning?" "No," the man replies, "why?" "You better put it on," Mudflap says.

They start the job. Soon they need the big truck. Off Mudflap goes with his help, listening to the radio. They stop for coffee along the way. In the coffee shop the TV is on, a line of people standing and staring at the burning towers, nobody saying a word.

The next two weeks that followed, everybody was extra nice to one another. But slowly everyone became numb from the constant barrage the media frenzy put out. They all returned to their more introverted behavior.

Now Mudflap and everyone around him is used to the constant talk of war and disaster, fear and crisis.

But there are puppies in the world.

Mudflap no longer had dogs. Each one lived a shorter and shorter life, till the last one never got a chance to grow up at all. While alone in his new house, he had no time to care for a dog. And the thought of another loss was too much for him to even contemplate.

The kids had fish; they were clean and easy. When Mudflap's daughter was about eight, they got rabbits. Dogs were out of the question. One day, when the daughter was ten, she was talking about puppies. She was pestering him. With a slip of the tongue, Mudflap said, "Maybe." That was it, non-stop! She would not come up for air, "Puppy, puppy, puppy." She sensed weakness and went in for the kill, relentlessly! Mudflap caved and said, "Yes, but I am choosing the dog."

He had seen a hybrid poodle mutt at a client's house. It looked like a Muppet, a scruffy ball that didn't shed. He no longer wanted a big dog messing up his nice clean house. The no-shedding thing sounded appealing. And poodles are wicked smart, so a "Cock-a-Poo" it was. A love puppy, a sweet ball of hair, buff colored. If you spray painted it blue, it would look like Cookie Monster. Mudflap wanted it to be a female - they don't roam. Her name was Ellie, or L. The dog was skeptical of everything, a real New Englander, and perfect for the family: only 22 pounds, perfect for travel to Maine. She never wanted to be left behind, first in the truck, first in the boat. She became family fast.

It was approaching twenty years since Mudflap had bought the farm. Puppies and 9/11 are the biggest events worth mentioning. There was no real drama to speak of. Beautiful days with the children, and the regular drama of every day work leave no memorable landmarks. The bad help, or crazy customers, are of little consequence and don't make interesting stories. Thank God. Mudflap cleaned up his life.

Karma rules. Mudflap saw it often. If someone wronged him, he would not start a big fight. His wife taught him passive aggressive tactics. But later on, without even asking, he would find out about the bad things that would happen to the rotten people who messed with him. Mudflap didn't have to swing; karma swung for him.

That doesn't mean Mudflap is a pushover. His sarcastic wit and the sharp tongue inherited from his mom can still strike quickly. He has learned by his own misery, no karmic debt goes unpaid.

And there is no such thing as coincidence.

Mudflap had been blamed by his brother and his wife for all the troubles caused back in the old days. Mudflap lived far across the river, and never visited after the mom was gone.

Taking Mudflap out of the situation didn't magically fix their life.

Long after Mudflap worked in Virginia, 26 or 27 years ago, his cousin showed up. He and his wife were taking a ride to New England. Mudflap had visited him a couple times with his family, going to D.C. and Smithsonian adventures. The cousin knew he had a farm in Maine. Mudflap didn't get the time off he would like. He was not at his farm that much. They surprised him with a visit, out of the blue.

The aunt down in Sebago was gone now too. Brother spent time in Maine, like the rest of the family, and had met his wife there. Brother and his wife had a camp not far from Mudflap's farm. They did have some times together, brother caming over with his son. But after mom's death they stopped coming.

Mudflap got a call from the police, they were looking for his sister-in-law. Mudflap got the call because he had the year-round house and was in the phone book. Brother was dead; fell off the waterfall in his backyard.

Mudflap gave the police their unlisted number, next thing you know the cousin is calling with his surprise visit.

The sister-in-law went back to Connecticut, put together a memorial service and neglected to tell Mudflap. But the news being too big, he was getting calls.

As soon as the cousin arrives, he and Mudflap leave and go back to Connecticut, getting there just in time for the service. The place is filled with all his brother's friends. One little row of Mudflap's people, his father- in-law, and two of mom's old friends: a neighbor lady, and the lady from the inn who had lost her daughter.

Mudflap's wife and the kids stay at the farm with the cousin's wife. Mudflap does not want to put them through the hectic mess.

The story was brother and friends were really tanking it up, drinking lots of beer and whisky, and he must have slipped in the dark by the waterfall. They left out the part that sister-in-law was in Maine with the kids, because they had a blowout; she wanted a divorce.

The Brother was about to lose his family, like he lost his father. They were calling it a drinking accident.

Mudflap didn't buy it at all, not for one second.

The Death of the Debt Monster

Remember the story of David and Goliath?

Perseverance and Wit can take down any Giant!

Mudflap, Over and Out !

Summer is here again, and Mudflap and family were on their way to Phoebe Island, kids and L in the back seat of the Silverado, the little green boat (Phoebe Too) in tow. Everyone was happy and full of anticipation for the fun to come.

The farm had been on and off the market now for the last 17 years. Mudflap was driving the realtors crazy. They just want a quick sale, he wants to be paid for his work. Every year he does a different project, expanding and renovating. The realtors just want him to drop the price. Mudflap feels that with every year that goes by, and every project he does, he is reinvesting, buying his own property so to speak.

The days of salesman/salesperson are mostly over. There are a few good ones left, but they are few and far between. The internet trashes industry after industry. Simple cab drivers have to fight against the guy down the street with a car and a couple extra hours on his hands. It's all non-stop crap, that's here to stay.

Want to see some blood and guts - wait till there are Uber tree cutters!

Realtors are greatly affected by the internet. Back before the internet, real estate got a sales slam from stay-at-home moms, whose husbands worked and paid the bills. When the kids started school, the moms, with more time on their hands, went to work selling real estate. (There is always the exception to the rule.) But these women were able to spend more time getting established with their bills paid, than a male counterpart who had to bring home the bacon, so to speak. Unfair to the men.

"You go, girl!" About time the discrimination was reversed!

But now the internet has made it worse for real estate, taking away the advantage even from those moms.

Any "Bozo" can sit back and click the mouse. And they do. There are no longer real estate salespeople, there are "mostly" real estate listers. Click and post people. (Again there are always exceptions.)

If they don't get a sale fast, it's "Drop the price!"

What they don't tell you is the internet is hit-and-miss. Mudflap has done direct searches on properties that he knows are out there, and they do not necessarily come up. Your listing can be lost in the many pages.

But if the realtors do not have their fast commission, you must drop your price!

And if it still doesn't sell, drop it even lower! Trashing the market. Add the greedy banking system, and we are all sucking wind - everybody with a house, even if you're not selling. Your equity line ability is affected ! ! !

Back at the farm, Mudflap had been between realtors, the farm was off for a while. He re-lists with a new broker at twice the price he started at, seventeen years and three recessions later.

Off the family goes, north to Sebec. Cell service is primitive, and there were not a lot of towers around.

Once set up at the island, they decide to take an unusual trip out of their regular way: to Acadia National Park. It's the most famous Maine park, but the kids have never seen it - always just tagging along on their dad's work/vacation trips. Mudflap has not been there for 20 years now, since his excursion with the infamous lady with six kids.

Acadia at the time was a cell phone dead zone. They disappear off the grid all day. On the way back to the Island, the old style bag phone (it was a full-size monster) comes alive!

There are 10 messages: where are you? The farm is sold at full asking price!

The Monster's Debris Field

The bigger they are, the harder they fall.

Some people really know how to make a mess.

So do not "Mess" with them!

Mudflap, Over and Out !

Mudflap for the last time sweeps the concrete floor of the Morton building that he had erected a decade earlier. The giant pole barn is 56' X 90' and has serviced him for years. The farm sale is a done deal. He has a month to clear out his property. The kids are back at the house with mother, he works alone, practically in tears, so relieved it's all over. He has time to reflect about all that has happened, a lot of good, as well as a lot of bad experiences over the 20 years. He is preparing the first wave of equipment for transport to Connecticut.

The one crew, one job-at-a-time system had paid off. Less income, less mistakes, less aggravation, more money at the bottom line.

With one guy, he could over pay him, better for the both of them. Instead of turn-over with help, they now stayed years. He had mechanics he could count on, trusting them with his life. He was no longer plagued with complaints from clients.

He was not getting anything at the closing that he could spend, every dime gone, but he was debt free.

The farm looked like something out of a postcard; that's why it sold. Mudflap made it look so natural it looked like it took care of itself, but he knew that was not true. He worked in the yard constantly. The mother had planted a clematis in the front. It grew and wrapped around the tree like mad. Damn thing never did bloom. The kids helped too, everyone had blood in the yard.

They were on the way back to the farm again, for the last haul, Mudflap was to meet the new owner. He planned to go around with him, showing him everything he had done, and tell him about things in the ground and under the buildings that no inspector could ever begin to figure out.

Mudflap was proud of all the work. He had collected so much after two decades, he couldn't haul it all away. He planned to leave the new owner lots of discretionary items. Not just because he couldn't haul it all away, but to be a good guy too.

The renters Mudflap had were gone, and the main farmhouse was spotless, so the new owner already could move in. Mudflap had in the contract a time limit to clean out the two barns and guesthouse.

The "little house" as they called it (the guesthouse) Mudflap had built for the family to use as they island-hopped. It wasn't very big, but neither were the kids; it was cozy. It was so small Mudflap wanted no junk in it. Everything was beautifully furnished and decorated, the beds made, all ready to go.

Mudflap learned one thing important over the 20 years: never leave a mess to come back to. He hated to clean up last time's crap. He always left the place spotless!

They were now again in Maine, almost off the highway, and Mudflap gets a call. (Here we go!)

The new owner is on the phone. He tells Mudflap: "I will be delayed for a few days, can't be there till Tuesday for the walk around. Oh, and by the way, I used the guesthouse."

"What?" Mudflap said. "You slept there?" "In my bed?"

"Yes," he replied. "It was all set up, so I used it." Mudflap was quiet, shock setting in.

Then he said, "See you Tuesday." "Ok," Mudflap replied.

With mouth hanging open, Mudflap hung up, and looked at his wife. She had been listening. "How bad could it be?" she said. Mudflap could feel his blood pressure spike! We are stopping at Walmart, and getting new sheets. Mudflap's wife thought he was over-reacting. She didn't want to bother with Walmart. Mudflap was adamant. "We are stopping."

Mudflap had over the years become increasingly fussy about a clean home and especially the bed. He loved nice sheets and comforters. He worked hard, got real dirty, and did not like to sleep in a mess. Period! And that's why he got a Cock-a-Poo: no shedding.

They finally got to the farm; the rest of the ride was no fun for Mudflap. He had been getting madder with every mile. The poor wife/mother knew Mudflap was not fun when you got him going. She could tell he was not happy at all.

They drove up to the little house and went right in. Usually they would walk around the yard and stretch a bit after a long ride.

Oh, my God! It was worse than they could ever have imagined. First, the place was in general disarray. He went right to the bed, turned back the comforter and saw blood all over the sheets, a complete mess. They sent the kids outside to play with the dog. The waste basket in the bathroom was full of bloody feminine napkins. The refrigerator was a mess too, leftovers thrown in with their condiments. Everything had to go. They had to go back out to the store, and spent an hour cleaning up the disaster.

Mudflap was ripped! He had never in his life felt so violated! His perfect little home, trashed!

This meant "War!"

It was Saturday afternoon. He had two and a half days before the new owner was going to be there.

The agenda had changed dramatically. They

went shopping. On the way they stopped at the antique store their friend had. Things Mudflap was going to leave for the guy were now going to be taken or given away. He told his friend to come help clean out the place. Things he had bought there were now being given back for free. Of course his buddy was on board.

They went and got a U-Haul. At the store, he told the counter guy about an old fiberglass canoe. It was heavy, Mudflap didn't want it. Gave it to the counterman, just come and get it. He showed up later the same day.

Mudflap blew through those barns like a madman, cleaned out everything of any great value.

One thing not mentioned: during this period Mudflap was badly hurt, and sporting a nasty knee injury.

He had hurt himself pulling wood from a river. That injury was agony for two years, and pain for two more. He never missed a day's work the whole time.

They loaded up the furniture from the little house, and camped on the floor Monday night.

Mudflap left anything with negative energy behind, not wanting any baggage from the 20 years of strife. He would never leave a watercraft. The canoe he gave away was not only heavy fiberglass, it came from a person who was mean to Mudflap. That's really why he gave it away. As he went through the buildings, all things he wanted to disassociate himself with were put in the center of the big pole barn. The reason he was doing this was just to keep everything separate from the things he wanted, with no other motive.

The pile grew. There were some Haitian artifacts he picked up along the way. Mudflap collected all sorts of things. Those artifacts were creeping him out; he didn't want them, so into the pile they went.

Tuesday morning early, he was ready to go, sure he was ahead of the new owner.

As his family loaded up their things, Mudflap took one last look in the barn. There had been so much grief and sadness at this property. He fought so hard all those years to make it right, putting much love and himself into everything there. There were ghosts there: his dogs, and lost family and friends, all the hard times. The old farmhouse had belonged to the grandparents of the neighbors from the OK Corral. There was always bad energy there Mudflap had to fight. He didn't want the place to begin with. But through it all he made it right. He made it a good place, and his family had happy times there, despite it all.

The violation of the buyer, the contempt and carelessness, the complete disregard for all Mudflap had done and been through was just too much.

He took the barn in one last time. Something

happened, somewhere, somehow: he started a ceremony. He did not know where it came from; it just flowed out of him. At the end he turned his back and walked to the door.

Stuck in the wood by the door was a large hawk feather. As he opened the door, he spotted it. He plucked it out, and as he left, the very last thing he did was wave the feather around in a circle, and gave it a little snap, like a whip.

With feather in hand he left.

The little convoy pulled away, the wife/mother driving the U-Haul, Mudflap in the Silverado with trailer.

On the way down the road his bag phone rang. It was the new owner saying he would be there soon. Mudflap told him, "Ok, see ya." He smiled, thinking about him showing up to no one.

The family still had their island in town. They would drive by the farm every once in a while, usually on the way home.

Mudflap noticed at first that it wasn't looking as good as he had kept it.

Every time he drove by, it looked worse.

A house was put in the side yard, near the Ok Corral. It looked out of place, ruined the yard.

Mudflap heard there was trouble at the town hall with the new owner. He chopped up the lots, making all the buildings separate.

The little house was its own lot, and the old barn lost its back field.

He was making a mess of the place.

The fall after the sale Mudflap had talked to his realtor. She told him the market was sliding down, he was lucky to have gotten the sale. He thought about that every time he went by.

Not long after, Mudflap heard at the town hall the property was under foreclosure.

The seasons passed, the place was looking like hell.

Mudflap stopped driving by, couldn't bear seeing the place anymore.

The years started to pass, the next people were making bigger messes. Mudflap was sorry he went by again.

The next time he passed by, they stopped and walked around because there were for sale signs posted. Mudflap felt like a ghost, the big pole barn was full of junk cars, and crap was everywhere.

The kids were now young adults. Mudflap, Mother and Daughter drove by after a big trip island hopping. They decided to swing by on the way out of town.

They got a real shock!

Just when you think it couldn't look worse. Mudflap drove up the road, the overgrown yard so thick he couldn't see the house. But there was the old barn. He stopped, backed up, but where was the house?

My God, it was gone !

They pulled over, got out.

The house was gone completely. Just some of the granite foundation stones, some charred wood, and debris were all that was left.

Mudflap's daughter said, "It's your fault. You jinxed the property."

The trees Mudflap planted were scorched too. It looked like a bomb had gone off.

They walked around in awe.

Mudflap went to pick up something, his daughter said, "Don't take anything." He stopped, knew she was right.

They started back to the truck. As they went by the tree where the mother had planted the clematis, Mudflap stopped in his tracks.

There in the disfigured tree was the biggest clematis flower Mudflap had ever seen.

Chapter 9

Islands Only

Pine

The whole point of an island is that it's all by itself.

A great place to be alone, even better with someone you love.

Leave it all behind, and don't forget to bring everything.

Mudflap, Over and Out !

It's the spring of 2006: Mudflap and family, with no farmhouse, access the island in Naples by marina only. It was a game they would play for the next seven years, parking in the center of town, right on the highway. They leave the truck and trailer across from the marina, and boat out, fully loaded with supplies for the week.

Mudflap seems to always end up on or off some state highway, his trips to Maine always a Road Warrior adventure. He may be on the side of the road, but he has lived in the area so long now he has connections. He knows his way around, and it's actually really easy for him. He has owned Pine Island now for a decade and has been working on it the whole time. He has finished the outbuildings, and installed a proper septic system. The main structure is rough still, but they can live there without a land base.

Naples is the center hot spot for the whole Sebago Lakes Region. The state highway Route 302 runs out of Portland to New Hampshire and the White Mountains. In the early spring and late fall, when boating out, Mudflap can see Mt. Washington snow capped right behind the island.

The Causeway, as it's called, has four marinas, restaurants, shops, pontoon plane rides, boat rentals, sport shops, the works. The family goes into town for supplies, and ice cream; it's a non-stop party.

Boat shows, motorcycles everywhere, antiques, fireworks, the kids love it. And their island is a five to ten minute boat ride from all the fun.

But then they escape the hectic mess, and retreat to their spot. Mudflap always called the Causeway the Naples Zoo.

Besides chasing off an occasional trespasser, there is very little drama. They swim and snorkel, have little spots to sit, and play lots of different games.

Mudflap and family continue to fuss over the island and take very good care of it. They dream of the day when they can afford to fix up the house. It's a bit of a shack. They sleep inside in a tent that they leave set up just like the old Phoebe. (You know Mudflap, he doesn't like sleeping in the dirt.)

They love the environment and are connected

to the Greater Powers that be.

Mudflap and family enjoy the peace.

Phoebe

**Phoebe was a Titan Goddess, Daughter to the
God of the "Sky" Uranus,
and Gaia Goddess of the "Earth"**

**She was the Greek Goddess of "Prophecy"
And was closely associated with the Oracle of
Delphi**

Grandmother to Apollo and Artemis

Don't play games with the Gods

Mudflap, Over and Out !

Phoebe Island is a completely different experience from Pine Island. It is a spiritual place where one can go to recharge and reconnect to one's own soul, as well as to the entire earth and universe.

Mudflap now understands why his Guardian guided him there. It was to bring the powers that be to his family, and to help him to repair the damages done to his soul, so he, too, would be grounded.

Dover-Foxcroft is the social hub of Sebec Lake. It's an Old New England industrial town that was somehow able to survive and do well during the economic changes of the region.

When you visit Dover, Mudflap's favorite grocery store is Will's. The people there are very nice. Not the I-want-something-from-you nice, like the

Connecticut crowd is skeptical of. It is more a sincere, polite, everyday nice. Little old ladies go by and smile at you like they are your own Granny. Everyone you interact with shows a common decency like the old times. Seems you're in a Leave it to Beaver, or a Father Knows Best show.

Not to say they don't have their share of people who have disdain for Flatlanders. People are people and they have their share of those who have prejudiced feelings too.

On the subject of Flatlanders or "People from Away" as they are also called: the guys Mudflap knows, who he hangs with around the lake, say that everybody south of Dexter is a Flatlander.

Naples is 150 miles south of Dexter. When Mudflap is down in Naples, and they start that Flatlander talk with him, he loves nothing better than to say in return, "You're a Flatlander and so is everybody south of Dexter where we go in Sebec. That's what I have been told." Then watch their faces as they take it in.

The trip to Sebec is seven hours from New Hartford. For that reason the family likes to island hop. Mudflap likes history, he collects items, and enjoys all sorts of history stories from every period. He often channels different times and different events.

The environment has the closest place in his heart. At Phoebe one does not have to catch nature. All you have to do is let nature catch you.

Sitting on the front stoop, Mudflap can observe an eagles' nest on another island in the channel. The adult eagles fly back and forth to the nest. The young eagles sit on the nesting tree's branches, and from time to time take flight and practice flying around the cove.

Hummingbirds battle over the feeders that Mudflap's wife sets up, multiple pairs challenging each other for possession and rights of the territory.

Loons pop up just a few feet away. They know it's a great fishing spot too.

A small raft of merganser ducks make their way by, usually traveling in groups of five or seven.

A heron fishes on the shore nearby.

A common duck and her group of young go paddling by in a cute, little, military-style row.

The osprey circles and swoops quickly through the scene.

If you're lucky, the kingfisher will make his appearance.

Waxwings and goldfinches fly in and bounce around in the blueberry bushes.

And dramatic sunsets complete the view.

All this happening and Mudflap hasn't left his chair.

Phoebe is quite the place, so close to shore the family walks off quickly up to their ponds, for another wildlife adventure. Every year the pond's landscape grows in thicker, and more wildlife moves in. Moose tracks have been spotted; they still wait to catch a glimpse of one.

When the pond was first dug, the family came up early that spring to plant grass, in a hurry to beat the erosion. Blood spilled down their foreheads as they contended with the black flies that came out early, too.

The harshness and raw beauty are why they are there.

Thunderstorms add to the drama. Choppy waves on a blustery day or dense fog in the morning make a spooky canoe ride.

When you catch the perfect glassy, mirror-style water, you must take advantage, the conditions change constantly.

The kids are growing up. The teen years are on the way.

The neighbors there are salt of the earth people. Many local Maine people have homes on this lake, as well as people from away. They know how to politely ignore you, but don't miss a trick.

It takes time to make friends in a place where isolation is coveted. Friendly as the area folk are, it's still New England.

The neighbor, from whom Mudflap obtained the right-of-way and land, sold his property and moved on to other adventures.

His favorite neighbors are still there, enjoying the lake year round. They get the place mostly to themselves all through the winter.

Time passes, it's always sad to say good-by for the season. Time to dream of another year around the corner.

Chapter 10

The Teens and Beyond

New Hartford

Eventually children reach that awkward stage when they are embarrassed by their parents.

**Why keep them in suspense?
Just get it over with!**

Mudflap, Over and Out !

Islands may be fun for the family, and nothing can compete with the experiences Phoebe has to offer, but New Hartford is Mudflap's home. The state highway is always out there, even though he tunes out the regular traffic, a motorcycle, loud truck, or police siren will not let him forget it's there.

The quaint main street, old homes, and churches are comforting to Mudflap as he returns home after a long day. His view of his own property as he pulls in is a mass of garden flowers all around the yard and a wrap-around porch that his wife planted and cares for. He loves his front yard, never forgetting the islands; they are just the back yard in his mind.

The state highway has its advantages. Besides the quick access which Mudflap uses during storms to save the world when trees attack, the highway offers the ability to quickly extinguish commodities of all sorts. If you don't want something, just put it out with a free sign and it's gone. If you have something bigger that's saleable, it's a great venue too.

When Mudflap's children were little, he was paranoid they would escape and get out into the road. The backyard was a high security zone, with fencing and obstacles. The home security system was more to keep people in than out; New Hartford has a low crime rate. It is as close to Mayberry and Dover as you can get in Connecticut, a great place to bring up children.

If you really want to hit the flatlands, Washington, D.C. is the way to go. Mudflap took his family on a couple of excursions to the Federal Mall with all the monuments and the Smithsonian buildings. Free for all citizens, all you have to do is get there.

On the way back they would stop at Gettysburg. If you want to talk ghosts, or the supernatural, that place has got them. If you're a person with high sensitivity to things you can't see, walking around there gives you goose bumps. The history-loving family enjoyed the walks there and stories of Little Round Top and the Devil's Den. If you can catch both D.C. and Gettysburg, they are great free activities. Mudflap likes free stuff.

The kids are getting bigger, and Mudflap takes his boy to civil war reenactments after Gettysburg. He doesn't want his daughter left out. Young boys are starting to take an interest in Mudflap's girl. Mudflap likes to rattle cages, enjoys a joke, and likes antiques. It's a perfect storm.

Mudflap acquires a full-scale antique field gun: beautiful black iron, goes perfectly in the front yard with the flowers, looks like a memorial. Gets the attention of the boys on the school bus. Now Mudflap's baby girl's dad is the guy with the cannon. She protests but it does her no good. It's still out there today, and at 24-years old his daughter is still Mudflap's baby.

As the years pass Mudflap's girl is the one to be on the wild side, starting to give him the payback karma demands.

Mudflap wanted to give his children all the advantages he never had. With all good intentions, it's the fault of so many of us in his generation. They all grew up with material limits, but didn't know it at the time.

Mudflap's kids grew up using free playscape stuff Mudflap would acquire out of yards he worked on. Glad he didn't pay for it all because they quickly outgrew things.

Mudflap to this day is in awe of the complex and elaborate playscape sets he sees in clients' yards, that very often the kids don't use much. The people often bought it more for themselves, because they never had such a thing.

A detail that may be hard for you to believe, now that you're getting to know Mudflap, but he has pet peeves!

A big peeve is, after he has quoted a tree removal, upon arriving to do the take down, a playscape has been erected in the way. The clients have spent so much on it they don't want him to even take it apart and get it out of the way. They would prefer he risks his life dangling on ropes, working around the over-priced toy, and at no extra charge to boot. "Right"!

Even better they park it under a tree, and then obsess over the branches above the toy nightmare.

Mudflap has walked away from many such situations.

As the playscape ages, it becomes a monument to the child's past, and can stay there for a time extended far past its useful life. Mudflap is alway eager to help people move on, and takes his chain saw to as many as he can.

Mudflap tried not to spoil his kids. His vacations to Maine were really work trips in disguise.

Mudflap's kids were the Yin and Yang. The boy, the introvert and studious, the girl outgoing and trade oriented.

Extreme bookends: one conservative and righteous, the other liberal and righteous too.

The boy was good and an excellent student through high school. Short story, no drama.

The girl, a free spirit, was smart but defiant to the system. Where would she ever get such an attitude? ! ! !

Nice stories aren't interesting. Mudflap's life might be good now. But it's not just about him at this point. Here is where we channel David Attenborough in the series *Life*. The quote was about birds as parents: The parent's purpose is to pass on genes, and then insure the survival of the next generation.

The adversity the bird went through just to mate, and then again the adversity it went through to ensure the survival of its young, is nothing any being would do in its right mind if its only concern was that of itself.

Mudflap's father was the exception to the rule. He was so self-absorbed that he didn't mind letting his family go hungry while he drove something extravagant like the pace car right off the track of the Indianapolis 500.

Even a polar bear father, who would eat his young if hungry enough, has a better reason for his action.

A good parent will instinctively do whatever it takes for his offspring, regardless of his 401(k), and under the bus we all go, not only for children, but for anyone in our lives who have meaning.

That idea opens up a big barn door, and people we help, like projects - and many are projects - don't always come out the way we imagined. Here is where we are all being a Mudflap. It can have great rewards or great sorrow.

This is where you, as project coordinator, have to make the judgment calls. Sometimes we need advice. We are intellectual creatures, not just wildlife. That's supposed to be the difference. Where I am going with this is a seminar put out by the high school, but in my rant I'm ahead of myself. Back to Mudflap.

Each kid got a free vehicle to start. Rural towns require vehicles to get anywhere. Mudflap realized this, and also realized the danger of the highway. He also is thrifty, and likes free stuff, but draws the line on having his kids driving junk cars.

The son got a well-maintained truck at the bottom rung of the fleet's ladder, safer than anything Mudflap ever drove at the same age.

Mudflap's baby got the best used car he ever bought in his life. That car collected dents like a magnet.

The first time she really banged it up, he got it fixed. He still kicks himself for not pocketing the insurance check. As it collected dents again, he made her ride them. When he put a triple layer of window screen in, to protect the radiator because she stuffed in the front, she had the nerve to complain, and demand a proper front grill. Mudflap thought it looked cool, like a stock car.

Then she had no concept of insurance. And neither did her older, supposedly wiser boyfriend. Without consulting Mudflap, all of a sudden the boyfriend was just driving around in the car. No big deal, only risking the entire cost of Mudflap's insurance on the whole fleet. No big deal, cars are free, aren't they? So is insurance, right? And the mechanic loves Mudflap; he works for free too. Right?

Mudflap was ok with the older boyfriend, thought it would mellow out the wild one. Turns out he was more spoiled than she was. Parents handed him everything. The world is free!

Mudflap was always good to his daughter's friends, did not want to see them all hanging out in parking lots, getting shaken down by the cops. So he gave them a haven at his place. The thanks Mudflap got was they kept him up on work nights, which is every night, making lots of noise to all hours.

Mudflap had to constantly scream down to them to "Shut up!" Bad as it was, he did sleep better knowing where she was.

When it was just girls, it was even worse. Three or four of them together sounded like a flock of birds in distress.

Mudflap wanted to be a better parent than lots

of parents he knew and grew up with. Saying no all the time is numbing to a child.

Back in the old neighborhood there was the meanest dad around. If his kids got out of line he took a coat hanger to them. Mudflap thought that was deplorable; his kinder and gentler mom would use only a belt: "The Strap" as she fondly referred to it. Stepdad never laid a hand on anyone, to any real consequence. The stepdad once threw Mudflap over his knee and started to spank him. He got mad when Mudflap laughed. It was nothing like a punch in the face.

Back to the meanest dad: Mr. Coat Hanger. He said no to everything, "No" matter what ! He was horrible! Mudflap knew he was a real back end of a horse, and swore he would never be that kinda dad.

Years later Mudflap saw Mr. Coat Hanger at his best friend's funeral. He was smoking outside, looked feeble, old and miserable. It gave Mudflap some satisfaction, karma was taking its toll.

On the other side of the coin of old neighborhood dads, there was Crazy Man's dad. One night Mudflap and another friend went over to see Craze, and he was not home. His dad answered the door. He saw their bags and he knew it was alcohol. Instead of turning them away into the night, he said, "Come in boys, don't sit in the bushes like bums, have a seat." He went to the cupboard and got Mudflap and friend a couple of glasses.

That dad, without reprimanding them, had the boys take a step up in self-esteem. That's parenting !

Saying no too much has an adverse effect on any child. You have to pick your battles. That's why Mudflap was a lenient father.

Mudflap was ripping mad at his daughter and her cavalier boyfriend, but did not say a word. He signed the car over to his daughter, and made her take out her own insurance policy.

She was mad to pay the $140 registration fee at the motor vehicle department. Mudflap laughed and said, "See, a free car still isn't really free; nothing is."

She finally had to push the limits of exhaustion, not wanting to get left out of the family traditions. She fell asleep and rolled the car over. Mudflap got the call at 3 a.m. As soon as the phone rang, he knew exactly who it was.

Luckily she drives slowly, and there were guardrails, so the car just kinda fell over and plopped on its roof.

She was less than ten minutes from home. She had been traveling back from New Hampshire. Mudflap was the first one on the scene. It was a lonely stretch of state road, on the back of a reservoir. If she had hit trees or gone down the embankment instead of the rails, nobody would have found her for a long time.

Coincidentally, she was the same distance from home as Mudflap had been with the cute little white Pinto with the blue vinyl top. The continuity of the two accidents is most likely due to the fact that being tired and fighting sleep becomes more dangerous the closer you get to home. Thinking you're almost there makes you drop your guard for just that one crucial second.

(So my tired driving friends, beware of those last few miles from home. Mudflap, Over and Out !)

When Mudflap arrived, his first sight was the car on its roof, right smack on the center line, sideways, taking up as much of the road as possible. His daughter was standing off to the side, straight faced, erect like a military guard on duty.

Mudflap cleaned out the car, double checking for any sketchy items, or contraband, loading up his truck as he went. He knew it was the last time he would ever see that car again, so he wanted it cleaned out properly.

Finally, what had to be at least forty minutes since the accident, a van with three workmen-looking guys came down the road. Mudflap told them he had it under control. They couldn't get by, so after they were sure everyone was all right, they turned around and left.

When he felt the scene was secure, he called in the state troopers for the mop up.

A bunch of good old boys showed up, all in good humor, just glad they were not scraping her up off the road.

People don't really think about what horrible things these poor guys find at accidents.

An EMT checked the daughter out, made extra sure she didn't have a concussion. She had clear eyes and a stiff upper lip. She was saving the breakdown for when she got home.

They were scheduled to go to Phoebe in a day or so. Mudflap told her not to worry; she would get a new car when they got home. They all had a nice extended time there, for everyone to recuperate.

One of the policemen who showed up at the accident had to be six foot six and two hundred eighty pounds, the biggest, scariest trooper Mudflap had ever seen. Should have been a poster boy for the whole force.

Mudflap felt like a hobbit standing next to him. Nice guy. He told Mudflap stories about being an MP, pulling drunk soldiers who were packing 45's out of bars, as they waited for the wrecker.

The next day Mudflap, wife, daughter, and daughter's boyfriend, took off for their Phoebe reconnect.

Mudflap always let his daughter include her

friends. He put up with a lot over the years.

Mudflap's leniency and letting things slide, even things other parents would never condone, got him respect. Respect that he never would have gotten had he been a hard ass.   Mudflap also got inside information, the kids trusting him, keeping Mudflap in the loop of things.   (Mudflap was in "deep cover.")

Leniency, and letting sketchy things slide, combined with that cannon in the front yard, not only got Mudflap respect, but put a little fear in their hearts. Not really being sure just what old Mudflap was capable of doing, if they dared cross him.

When the family got home from Maine, Mudflap sent the daughter shopping for a vehicle.

Coincidentally, summer-season-end-clearance-sales were in full swing.

Mudflap got her into a brand new ride, with zero-percent financing and not a penny out of his pocket at closing.

He handed his daughter the payment schedule. It was time she learned what the cost of a vehicle really was.

She protested, and still does. But she is paying off that ride.

Mudflap, Over and Out !

The Road of Life

A Poem

The road of life does not go in a straight line; it is also
not a flat line.
It has hills and valleys, there are turns and forks.

Going up and down can be tricky; you do not want to
pick up too much speed
at the bottom, or not have enough momentum to
make the top.

The turns can be dangerous, and the forks do not
always go in the
direction we want to go.

There are guides in the road, helping you see your
way.
There are also obstacles and fog obstructing your
vision, making you go again
to places you may not want to be.

The easiest way most often leads you astray, but
sometimes the easy road
is the right one to take, if you know the short cut.

The right decision gets you to that place you want to
be.
The wrong decision could lead you away and you
may never,
ever see your destination at all.

There are forces, like magnetic fields, drawing you
down different
side streets, to places good and bad.

Circles that go around, back to the same place, or
dead ends where you
have no choice but to turn back.

Fuel in the form of karma is a driving force, helping
propel you along your way.
Contamination like water and dirt in your fuel can kill
your engine,
leaving you stuck somewhere you do not want to be.

The lucky few get a free ride; sometimes that free ride
has an unforeseen cost.
The best thing is to only take that free ride if you really
need it.
It usually works out better for you if you pay your own
way.

There are tolls, tickets, parking fees, and breakdown
costs.
Debts on your ride and payments, high prices out of
your control.

You come along the way to help others, some come
to help you.
There are some you should pass by and leave there,
and some you really should save.

Some do not really need help and fool you, and some
have just
plain lost their way.
.
Often you cannot tell the difference.
But their cost you absorb may forever haunt you.
That cost may be there to stay.

Finally I say, the good karma you create may not save
you
as you go on your way.

Watch out for that crazy guy out of control.
Who is out to ruin your day !

Mudflap's advice is:
Keep your destination clear and your fuel clean !
Over and Out !

Part 2

The Quiet Time

**Not often do hardworking middle-class people really
get a break for any great length of time.**

They all just have moments that they steal back.

Mudflap, Over and Out !

A new spring arrives. The difference between this spring and last is that Mudflap breathes the fresh air of freedom. The Debt Monster is dead.

The children are still young. The family goes to Maine without the extra burden of friends tagging along.

These are the last precious times the four of them get to spend together alone. The children are slipping away into that awkward pre-adulthood.

That sweet little innocence of that fragile family time is slowly fading away.

Mudflap's knee is feeling better, but he is still in pain all the time. He has learned to walk differently. He no longer runs at all, every step is now more carefully anticipated. No more zigzag maneuvers, like a squirrel in the road.

Ellie the dog has become a solid member of the family. Her quirky ways delight the happy group.

She is timid and skeptical of everyone and everything she meets. Inanimate objects startle her, still not trusting that fire hydrant in front of the next door neighbors' house, even though it's on her regular daily route to the post office.

Mudflap's tree service is becoming a more refined finish company. His past more destructive jobs are less and less his focus. He has an eye for beauty and scale. The properties he works on reflect the intuition he has for growth patterns of different trees and shrubs.

Every day is still a challenge for Mudflap and everyone in the tree industry. Weather, equipment issues, physical strife, and catering to the everyday whims of clients and the help, is a constant juggle.

Mudflap, who is used to adversity, thrives in the volatile, sometimes hostile daily environment, the weather and pain being a constant issue.

There are actually very few days when the sun is shining, the temperature is mild, and there is no wind or pain to nag him. Those days must be enjoyed, because they are so few and far between.

The children and mother are well adjusted into New Hartford's tight little social climate. It's a real New England experience, and being born there the children will never be called, "people from away."

The island-hopping adventures are in their hearts every day, the experiences attached to their personalities.

They get a few years of real solid grounding: the fun and excitement of the Pine Island Causeway and the whole Naples Zoo, and the complete interaction with Mother Earth at the Phoebe Island and the Wildlife Sanctuary.

Mudflap's fondest memory is snorkeling in the cove with his daughter, the water crystal clear, and the sun on their backs. As they were holding hands, Mudflap watched their shadows reflecting, fluttering like apparitions, across the rocks all so clear at the bottom.

Still holding hands they followed those apparitions around for a long time, the most spiritual experience of his entire life.

Mudflap felt the good energy flowing through his whole body, healing him right down into his core.

Spirals and Circles

Energy swirls around us with intensity unseen.

**Electricity is invisible. We see only our
environment react to it
in the form of sparks and lightening.**

**Voltage can light up your life, or can kill you.
The choice is yours how you handle it.**

**It can sneak up on you, if you are not aware,
and give you a good snap, or worse.**

**Better not hang out in thunder storms
if your karma is dirty !**

Mudflap, Over and Out !

The energy flows around us, spirals upward and downward, and in interconnecting circles. When these interconnecting circles come around and meet, we refer to that phenomenon as a coincidence. It's not that Mudflap does not believe in them, it's more he feels they are not properly defined.

Mudflap's girl, "The Wild One" came back around to her true inner-self. She's still wild like her dad, but in a more refined way. Her deep connection to the environment and Mother Earth, nurtured by her father and his love and appreciation of the natural world around them, grounded her.

She is a massage therapist, Reiki practitioner, and yoga teacher. She makes all-natural remedies, moisturizers and other contaminate-free products.

By guiding her in the right direction, rather than forcing her, she more quickly came to the right conclusions herself, raising her self-esteem even higher. When anyone tries to tell her what to do, Mudflap laughs.

Mudflap cleaned up his karma, realizing many of his troubles were due to fighting forces around him that in reality he should have just avoided. Even though he thought he wisely picked his battles, some were unnecessary, taking away energy and resources from battles more worthy.

Mudflap is an old soul, and old warriors die hard.

There are always new causes, and new fights to be won.
The day you stop fighting, old age has begun.

Pick them wisely !

Mudflap, Over and Out !

The Troll Under the Bridge

Trolls are from Scandinavian Mythology, very strong but stupid.
The sound of church bells drives them away.
Often afraid of sunlight, it can turn them into stone.
Primitive chaps that should be avoided, causing trouble with travelers.

The Gods don't bother with them, but they are a pest to men.

If you are a Troll don't bother the Gods; they are not looking for trouble.

But be careful, Troll. If it's trouble you're looking for,
you will find it !

Mudflap, Over and Out !

Spring turns towards summer, Memorial Day and island-hopping again take over the family's life. The breaks in the schedule are good for Mudflap's mental health, but can be more physically demanding than the tree work schedule.

Doing property projects as well as trailering boats and equipment, dealing with luggage, food and other supplies, like gas cans, fresh drinking water, tools and all sorts of items. Mudflap often is glad to get back so he can rest and just cut trees.

Pine Island is still a big project. Keeping up with the annual dead fall of debris from winter, and opening and closing the water system, and general all-around cleanup are the minimum Mudflap has to contend with.

Phoebe Island is the only real break he gets. The house is small, finished and easy to care for. But he still has to lug all the gear out. Thank God the kids are becoming a help too. Mudflap and mother used to have to lug them as well.

And thanks to the proper right-of-way deal Mudflap made with his friend on shore, everything runs smoothly.

Mudflap arrives at Sebec Lake, after the three-hour drive from Naples, where they just left Pine Island. The family as a team exits Pine, loading the boat and leaving the camp in good order. Mudflap doesn't want to return to a mess.

This is how the morning starts: Ellie, as soon as she sees gear being loaded, is the first to take her seat, waiting patiently, watching every move the family makes.

Mudflap channels the logistic talents of his long-dead uncle, who was a C.B. in the Pacific theater WWII. He knew how to island-hop.

They make the marina before 8 a.m. and the daily traffic, load the boat on the trailer and head out.

The coffee shop is the first stop. The last chore before leaving Naples and the three-hour ride to Sebec is to fill the five-gallon drinking water jugs at the local community well.

A grueling pace to keep, it's a real Mudflap vacation.

Pit stops and gasoline, before stopping at Dover. Next stop, Will's for food and ice.

Around the lake to the boat launch closest to Phoebe, with the pontoon boat fully loaded, Mudflap and son take the boat with Ellie perched at the bow.

The mother drives the boat and trailer around to the right-of-way. Mother and daughter have to take a rowboat across to the island. The dock/walkway is still in the storage container.

They all meet at the island. Mudflap secures the boat, and the unloading process begins.

The girls sweep up the flies and dust down the camp, as Mudflap and son lug gear, food and the water.

The family finishes setting up the house as Mudflap reinstalls the water line into the lake for domestic use, and turns on the water system. Turning on the gas for the stove is his last chore.

All this is finished before dinner, finally a break, time for evening relaxing and the first sunset of their stay.

One hectic day, but now they are ready for some real fun. Everyone sleeps well.

The next day the family got to meet the new neighbor, who has purchased the property where Mudflap has the right-of-way.

The neighbor is a retired captain of an ocean-going boat. The Captain was in command of a large ship. He was a real big shot.

The Captain invites the family over for drinks at happy hour time. Mudflap at this point in his life is dry. It's been around 20 years now since those days of extreme stress. Mudflap has worked hard to straighten out his life. He's not up for even a social drink. He senses the Captain's disappointment when Mudflap chooses an alcohol-free beverage at the little affair.

The Captain generously offers up use of his garage area and water hose so that Mudflap can flush out his boat engine. The Captain fears there could be microscopic pieces of invasive plant life hiding in Mudflap's water pump, because he had his boat in the southern lakes where Milfoil is a problem.

There is protocol for boaters to inspect their boats and trailers for any plant life snagged onto their equipment, during entry or exit to and from the lakes. All plant life is to be removed if spotted, regardless of whether it's an invasive plant or not. Removing all plants is the way to make sure no invasive species move around, because it can be difficult to identify such plants.

It is not required to flush out your engine for the reason of invasive plants. And nobody does.

Mudflap was taken aback. He said thank you for the offer, and left it at that.

An ominous feeling swept over Mudflap. This guy is trouble, he thought. This is a bad neighbor. My little paradise is in jeopardy. (Here we go !)

Mudflap tried to brush off the feeling, but it stayed with him the rest of that day, that week, and into the next year.

Bowerbank is the name of the town on the opposite side of the lake from Dover. It's as about as small as a town can get, with only 96 year-round residents, last time Mudflap checked.

It's so small there is no school; the few kids in town have to go around the lake to Dover.

There is only one town road: the Bowerbank Road. All others off this road are privately maintained.

Like many towns these days they have a town field day. Bowerbank Days are once every five years.

The Phoebe Island is in the town of

Bowerbank, as back woods and rural as you can get, even for Maine.

Mudflap really likes Bowerbank, and the way they all love their privacy and freedom. They are friendly like Dover, but more reclusive. There is a common feeling a lot like in Connecticut: be friendly, but mind your own business. They don't want you in their kitchen at night - give them space. But they will be there for you in a flash; you can count on them to save you in a pinch.

At Bowerbank Day there was lots of country fun: Bowerbank hats, tee shirts, and sweat shirts for sale; burgers and dogs on the grill; and an axe-throwing contest, etc.

The town was on a campaign of up-grading the road signs on all the camp roads, replacing the old wooden posts with the new style reflective green and white letters, more EMT friendly. It was almost impossible to see the old posts at night, especially when rainy or foggy.

Mudflap and family attended Bowerbank Day. Mudflap entered the axe-throwing contest. It was a full-sized, long-handled, double-bladed axe. Everyone in the contest used both hands to throw the awkward tool: swinging down first to gain momentum, then back over their heads, then releasing to the target 30 feet away. Everybody got two shots. The first contestants all stuck the axe in the target. No bull's-eyes though. Mudflap came up to take his turn. He was the only one to use one hand with the large tool. It was heavy even for the tough Mudflap. He was able to throw it, but it bounced off the top of the target. The second time he concentrated hard, everyone watching, the Captain included. He swung the tool again with one hand, and Bull's-Eye !

Mudflap threw a perfect shot, but was eliminated from the final round due to his not sticking it in both times. He walked away, happy with himself. Felt he really was the one who won, but never said a word. (till now)

At the table where they were selling Bowerbank clothes, a section was set up for house number signs, too. A little paperwork write-up the town put together said: Put the number on your house. If you can't see the house from the road, put the number at the end of your driveway or right-of-way.

Phoebe Island was designated #10. Mudflap bought the house number, as well as hats, sweats and tee shirts for the family.

Mudflap had only a parking lot on the land, no buildings. He couldn't afford more structures, and his time for financing everything he wanted was over. He had become anti-debt. Mudflap had a plan.

He couldn't tow his pontoon and the little green boat at the same time. He also had an aluminum staging plank walkway he used to access the island, but had to trailer that, too.

The solution was a 40-foot shipping container. Mudflap had plenty of room on his land. For less than the cost of a foundation, he could store his little boat and the walkway out of the weather year-round. It was a quantum leap in easy access equipment. He wouldn't have to tow a trailer at all anymore if he didn't want to.

He ordered it up and it was there faster than any building could have ever have been organized.

The Captain didn't like it.

And Mudflap never checked in with him to go through his boat flushing and inspection process.

Mudflap tried to politely ignore the Captain. He had stopped Mudflap a couple of times to talk, but the conversation turned to complaints about the locals, and the contractors over-priced construction costs.

The Captain felt all the contractors in the area were taking advantage of him.

Mudflap was a contractor; he knew the cost of doing business. He didn't want to hear the whining.

The Captain told Mudflap he didn't like the container. He said, "You should know better being from Connecticut. You shouldn't act like these people."

Well, Mudflap didn't know better. As a matter of fact, he liked the container. He was just as big a redneck as any of the locals, maybe worse. Mudflap didn't like the Captain trashing the locals, or his boat inspection ideas.

Mudflap bit his tongue. He really tried to be cool, just wanting to slide through and mind his own business.

Early morning was chore time at Phoebe. Mudflap would work doing some kinda maintenance, fussing over the landscape by the ponds and puttering around until it stopped being fun. Then it was time to swim, or sit back with a summer read - anything but work. He tried to keep a balance, so he was not scrambling to get things done at the end of the stay.

Mudflap took a treated 2 x 4 and a little board and put his house numbers on it. And as instructed in the town paperwork, put it up at the end of the road. It was at the beginning of the Captain's driveway, right where Mudflap was suppose to walk down the edge of the property line in his right-of-way.

It was perfectly placed so it was out of the way, but clearly guided anyone, EMT or visitor, towards the path down to the lake and the island.

The Captain short-circuited! Tore up the post and smashed the sign on the ground, breaking it.

When Mudflap went by with his family and noticed the broken sign, he asked what happened? The Captain got tough with Mudflap, and demeaned him in front of his wife and children. They argued about the right to have the house number.

Finally frustrated with Mudflap, he said, "Come on, tough guy." He put up his fists and said, "Let's go." Mudflap was not going there.

First of all, he saw through the Captain's motive. He knew he did not like the right-of-way. And violence could jeopardize Mudflap's access.

Second: Mudflap hadn't been in a fist fight since his brother and wife tag teamed him 26 years or more ago.

Third: Mudflap still had a bum knee and other aches and pains. He couldn't afford to get hurt; he needed his body to cut trees.

Mudflap called the sheriff's department reluctantly, knowing that often in domestic violence issues, both parties get arrested.

The sheriff was not happy with either the Captain or Mudflap. That fact was no surprise.

Since the sheriff did not do anything about the Captain's behavior, it empowered him to keep up his harassment.

Over the following seasons, the Captain would continue to harass Mudflap

Instead of parking next to his house for his own

easy access, he went out of his way to park both his vehicles in Mudflap's path.

One season he moored his boat right in front of Mudflap' s house, ruining the view, and the swimming as well. A captain should know Harbor Master rules. It was not only rude, but illegal, too.

He did lots of petty things.

Mudflap and his family were quiet and respectful neighbors, hardly there enough to bother anyone.

The greedy Captain was there all summer and wanted to ruin the couple of weeks the Mudflap family had.

Then the Captain thought he was channeling his redneck side. Thought he was cool, and started talking about having the right to shoot Mudflap because he was on his land.

Then one day while Mudflap was loading gear into his truck, the Captain came out, holding a rifle across his chest in the ready position. He looked at Mudflap. For that instant Mudflap was startled.

Then a little kid came up behind him. The Captain put the rifle down, and proceeded to walk out and hang a can on a tree about 30 feet away from Mudflap.

Then he started to help the little boy target

practice, shooting out of the garage.

Mudflap contacted the sheriff again. He came out and had a talk with the Captain after Mudflap left for the season.

The Captain lied to the sheriff.

He plays games with Mudflap, and does the best he can to spoil everybody's time.

The good neighbors got fed up, too. Like the sheriff, they didn't want to hear it.

Mudflap spent the next years putting up with the Captain until his son got out of college and his daughter was in her twenties.

The Captain thumbs his nose at the Powers That Be and keeps building up a big debt to karma.

He thinks he is the Captain of the lake, but he is the Troll under the bridge.

The Boy

As the young buck grows more points on his horns, he starts to feel the need to show them off.

The full-sized old buck has no desire to lock racks with the little one. He's too busy minding the herd.

Watch out with those horns, little buck, you could hurt someone. You're only scratching at the big buck. It's you who are going to get a good poke in the ass.

Mudflap, Over and Out !

When their boy was born, Mudflap and mother were very happy parents. They thought he was wonderful. Mudflap would raise him slowly above his head, and he would spread his little arms, balancing as he looked down with a sweet smile. They laughed and thought he looked like the baby Jesus himself.

He was a good boy and loved games of all sorts as he grew up. Food was less his focus, unlike his sister who was a little treat monster, and grew tired of games quickly. They got along fine, but were truly the proverbial Yin and Yang.

You haven't heard much about the boy, because his blissful life and good behavior don't make for an interesting story. A good thing, Mudflap worked hard to protect his family and spare them the perils of the world for as long as he could.

The farm experience for the boy was an enchanting world with all sorts of great places to play. The swampland in the thick old growth, way back in the woods he called "Dagobah" after Yoda's home in the *Star Wars* story.

Mudflap used the farm over the years to leverage him into all his other properties, always accessing the equity as he went along, trying to sell it every year. (You know the story.)

More about the boy in a minute, Mudflap's got another neighbor story for you. Not quite as dramatic as the Captain or the OK Corral, but it's a good one, too.

Remember: Contractors are a persecuted group, when it comes to neighbors. As you recall, they do stuff; they don't just go in their house and watch TV.

That's why Mudflap likes the Bowerbank crowd. Many are self-employed, and they believe you should be able to do what you want on your own land, and have the right to be left alone.

In New Hartford, Mudflap, true to his form, was stressing out the neighbors with his equipment. It really was not a big mess, just a fewthings, but anything is a bad thing if it's owned by the dreaded contractor.

So to be a good neighbor and because he liked the up-scale homes on Main Street, he bought a little shack of a place up by West Hill Lake, to take the pressure off his neighbors downtown.

It was a scruffy little neighborhood of old camp homes, all with an association that provided lake rights to a beach and docking system.

The little shack came with a generous-sized lot, and a year-round well. Most of the neighbors were seasonal, and Mudflap went to Maine more in the warm weather. He could put a few things in the woods there, out of everyone's way, and hardly ever be there to make noise. Mudflap thought it was perfect for everybody.

Mudflap decided to build a small garage, not unlike any size building in the neighborhood. But the old camp lots were non-conforming to new regulations and setbacks. Mudflap applied for a setback variance for his garage at the town hall. It was to be a conservative, low cost project that fit the neighborhood well.

Each abutting neighbor had to be notified.

Word spread, a tree cutter was building a garage. The dreaded contractor was going to bring in trucks and equipment and drag the scruffy, low-end neighborhood of trashy little, unkempt homes down into the depths of the contracting world.

The reality was that Mudflap had a place for his

big trucks at his mechanic's, closer to his jobs, and didn't want to climb the hill with his equipment. It was to be a garage for smaller equipment, a shop to get out of the snow and rain, and a place to do maintenance on the off days. Occasionally a bigger piece of equipment might show up, but Mudflap's intention was just to take the pressure off Main Street.

The whole neighborhood short-circuited. At the variance hearing, the room was packed, and there was a line right out the door of the town hall. The tree cutter must be stopped at all costs. Mudflap couldn't believe his eyes as he made his way through the tightly-packed crowd to his place at the hearing table.

After the fifth person got up to belly ache how horrible Mudflap was to even contemplate a garage, and looking at the whole line of people waiting to come up and have their say, Mudflap got up and walked out.

The next day Mudflap went back to the town hall to re-evaluate the garage project.

Town code officers usually don't give you advice, they just say yes or no to your ideas.

The zoning officer, whose job it was to regulate setbacks, gave Mudflap advice. He was mad at the neighbors, too, for making such a fuss. They really did not understand what they were talking about.

He told Mudflap to attach his garage to the house, then the existing sheds would become the setback line.

Attached, he could also put on a second floor. The detached proposal was for a much smaller building.

Mudflap did not appreciate the neighbors ganging up on him. He still remembered clearly being ganged up on before. He did not like the déjà vu moment. The second floor thing was very appealing as it doubled the floor space for very little extra cost.

The only problem was the whole property had to change to accommodate the building. If he was going this far, might as well make it big as you can, thought Mudflap.

Instead of a cute little garage in the woods, a building scaled to the neighborhood, Mudflap put up a monster-size barn.

Mudflap put up a 30 x 60 foot building, 30 plus feet high with white siding.

The teachers next door, who were first to complain at the meeting, didn't do their homework. The 20-foot high x 60-foot white wall was so close to their house, that they now needed sunglasses to contend with the glare bouncing off the building.

Because the lot was not level enough to accommodate such a structure, every tree on the lot had to go.

The neighbor on the opposite side of the property made the mistake of moving Mudflap's property line stakes around, and started putting garbage in Mudflap's woods.

When they leveled the lot, that neighbor got a wall of dirt on his line as high as the excavator could make it. Mudflap put up a heavy-duty wire fence there too, with silt fencing wrapped in it.

The neighbor did not like the silt fencing material and cut holes in it. Big, nasty bull briars have grown through the fence. It now looks like something out of a WWI battle zone.

It's now been 17 years since the barn went up. Mudflap pays his association dues, but does not hang out at the beach with the sore neighbors. But his daughter and wife use the beach passes regularly.

Mudflap is very happy with his big barn, especially the second floor. He has a nice sunset view.

The neighbors like Mudflap's daughter. She turned out to be so sweet and wonderful that everyone does. Now they are nicer to Mudflap, too.

They never did see much tree equipment; anything that visits there goes inside. They should have just left Mudflap alone.

Mudflap and his son had many good times in the barn before he went off to college.

The son was really good at math and toward the end of his junior year there was a college seminar at the high school.

Remember back some chapters ago, I was on a rant and mentioned a seminar. Well, let me tell you about the advice a professional college financial advisor told us all.

She said that if you are financially challenged and have no assets to attach, college for your child will be free.

If you have no money in the bank, but own a home with any equity at all, you must give it away into the system.

You can try to get a bunch of little Stafford type loans. Lower interest loans are available if you qualify. If you have a lot of equity in your house, you will not qualify for the lower rate deal. You will have to grovel and scrape to put all you have into the college tuition. She said, "Forget about a new car or a roof on your house. All the money you have must go into the college system."

She went on to say your kids can get cheaper college loans than you can, but you are still responsible for the debt. If you are a man who is a stepfather, you are responsible for the debts of the stepchildren, not their real father; he is off the hook completely.

She went on to say, "Don't touch your

retirement fund, that's a no-no." Even though the interest you pay on a loan may be more than you're making in the market. If there are grandparents with money to access, they will be responsible, too.

She went on to preach the doom and gloom. Some of that information Mudflap found later to be questionable.

The bottom line was that Mudflap was to be back in debt, his home in the clutches of the bank again, even though his knees still hurt, and his back, too. He was one injury way from being disabled, losing everything and being in the street, with his family in tow. But the colleges didn't care about his future or his health; they just wanted all the money they could shake out of him.

The college finance lady made the "Blood Sucking Divorce Lawyers", look fair. At least you knew they were stealing your money. The college lady said it was your duty to your child.

Mudflap was too busy to runaround getting 15 different loans, and was not letting the bank get a hold of any of his properties. They were his only chance to ever retire.

So he chose the no-no, and to stay debt-free, he cashed out his small retirement account. It would be just enough to pay for the state school, and UConn had a good actuarial program. It was the best shot for his son to get a good job.

Mudflap was not going to let his son down, and he had one more year before he was getting out of high school. One thing for sure, Mudflap was going to make his son's senior year a good time.

One final note on neighbors:

Mudflap always wonders why neighbors are so worried about what the next guy is doing with his land. The more you leave your neighbor alone, just like the kids, the more respect you are going to get.

Mudflap's barn on West Hill is the best looking building in the whole neighborhood, and he still got guff from the neighbors.

He puts a container on a 22-acre plot in the woods of Maine, and a neighbor doesn't like that either.

Go Figure !   Mudflap, Over and Out !

The Boy part 2

The financial advisor at the high school-offered seminar misrepresented the liabilities of parents, and did not more openly discuss options available.

No cute saying can fix that deception.

Today's press exposing the college greed is now helping everyone.

Do your research, don't let anyone rush you.

Mudflap, Over and Out !

Mudflap made a big mistake, being too worried about his boy, and less worried about himself. He should have questioned the advice of the seminar lady, and made his son do more.

In retrospect it was completely Mudflap's fault for the damage done to his long-term finances.

Mudflap spoiled the boy, trying to make his life as easy and as fun as he could.

Mudflap spent as much time as he could with his boy during his last year in high school. They started collecting old military firearms, daggers, and other military and historical items.

They went target shooting, trap and field, and all sorts of outings on Saturdays.

Mudflap had his son's friends up to Maine and Pine Island, and catered to all the kids.

Mudflap and son bonded and were good friends.

The years in college isolated the boy, spending too many hours alone, cooped up in the prison-type dorm room. When he finished his dual degree of actuarial science and finance, he came home a different person.

First thing Mudflap noticed was how adversarial he was at his first dinner home. Mudflap brushed it off as a young buck.

The boy got a job right way at a local insurance company. Everything was good; they had a solid family finance plan.

At the same time, daughter and spoiled boyfriend who thought the world was free, created drama within the family dynamic.

(Daughter got wise, and got rid of Free Boy)

It's easy to talk about the tragic life Mudflap endured for so many years. Lessons he was taught, and lessons he taught others.

The boy is a story that cannot be told.

Mudflap takes full responsibility for giving his son too much and spoiling him.

Old saying is old for a reason: "A son is a son until he takes a wife, and a daughter is a daughter all of her life."

Mudflap chooses a quote from his estranged son and another from his daughter-in-law.

First Quote: Daughter-in-Law, "Your son works so hard. All you do is cut a tree down and make $1,000."

Last Quote: Son, "I am not going to be stupid like you. I am saving for my retirement."

Chapter 11

The Fallout

Fallout can be something as simple as a disagreement.
or
It can also refer to the aftermath of a nuclear explosion.

Sometimes the simpler version can feel as bad as the extreme one !

Mudflap, Over and Out !

(The loss of the young buck weighs heavily on the does, the old buck leads the herd on.)

It's no longer the past, Mudflap marches into the future, with quite a few fronts to fight on. He faces his challenges as the lone buck in the herd. Without him, his women are in big trouble; they cannot face the obstacles before the family without Mudflap.

He is now sixty years old, and must focus on wrapping up his estate into a manageable situation. A tough old guy still climbing trees, and hopping islands, but the milepost of his age weighs heavily on his mind and future.

The tree service has become the simplest and most happy place Mudflap has to be. His right-hand man has been with him for an entire decade now. He is Mudflap's best friend.

His clients are the best of the best; he no longer has to cater to the demands of the general public. He has enough to do in the properties he enjoys the most and only works for people who he is truly fond of.

Motorcycles long ago were put on the back burner, time with family being more important. Mudflap sold his collection of bikes long ago. He kept his old 900, the favorite, and just parked it in the barn.

He walks by it all the time, watching the paint bubble on the tank and rust pits growing on the chrome. To Mudflap it is like the picture of Dorian Grey aging in the attic. He enjoys watching it deteriorate, as he recalls how so many times he rode it with his life hanging on the thinnest of threads.

He never maintained the 900 because he felt when he was ready, and had the time to ride again, he would buy the state-of-the-art bike of the times. Now with distracted drivers everywhere on cell phones, he would never dare ride a street bike ever again.

The Islands, once his biggest joy other than his family, are becoming his biggest burden. Each island has different challenges.

Pine Island, the party spot, and the Naples Zoo are four hours away. Mudflap was trying to sell the island without doing the renovation of the main structure.

Funny how little things can have a big impact. Mudflap can be superstitious, especially about natural environmental signs.

Nocturnal flying squirrels have moved into the house. The way the old building is constructed, and with its aging issues, it's impossible to keep them out.

And Mudflap will not kill them; it would be very bad luck. Besides, they are very cute and he likes them a lot. Seeing them glide between the trees come sunset is really cool.

The only solution is to knock the old house down and do the rebuild. He has a good friend in Naples ready to start the project this summer. It's going to take everything Mudflap has to start the project, and will take him three years because of the limits of his funds. Once the island house is finished, it will be very easy to sell.

The enchanting island experience Mudflap had is no longer. He now feels like Alice in Wonderland; he is being sucked down the rabbit hole. The only way out is forward; there is no going back.

Phoebe Island is seven hours away. Two seasons have passed with drama.

Season #1: After the sheriff gave the Captain a visit, there was some drama. The following chain of events happened:

Captain Troll created a blockade with his

vehicles, making it as unpleasant as possible for the family to go through the right-of-way.   Then he demanded Mudflap reconfigure his access point of entry.

Mudflap went along with the demand even though the established point of entry was better, and by rights he could have fought it. Mudflap was not up for getting shot for taking a canoe ride, so he agreed.

An armistice so to speak was called and there was a peace.

Mudflap started building a little cabin by the pond for extended families and future guests.

A tragedy occurred: Ellie the pup, 13 years old, died at the island of cancer. They brought her to the island in denial thinking she would make it to Christmas.

The heartbroken family buried her at the pond. She went out like a saint in a sheet. The little procession of Mudflap, mother, daughter, and daughter's boyfriend, carried the pup to the pond.

Mudflap dug a spot while everyone else gathered rocks to top off the grave.

The two weeks that followed their stay was tainted by heartbreak.

When Mudflap got back to Connecticut, he lasted one day, until he canceled his late afternoon appointments and went across the state to get another Cock-a -poo he found on line. He drove home in tears with the new puppy in his lap.

The dog is white and black and named Lucy. Mudflap calls her LuLu.

The family loves her and she helps everyone heal.

Season #2: Captain Troll is calm for the moment; the armistice is holding.

The annual fireworks freak out LuLu; she runs off the island into the dark. She keeps running and doesn't come back. After a sleepless night, Mudflap calls the sheriff's county office. With much relief, the family gets Lulu back two hours later.

Mudflap is now sporting a hernia, and has to be careful. He lifts docking and walkway planks, hauls gear and keeps going. He has to try and make it to the end of the season, plans to get the operation in January.

Towards the end of the stay, Mudflap contracts a realtor. After losing Ellie, dealing with his hernia, and almost losing LuLu, he's burning out.

Captain Troll does not want Mudflap to sell.

He calls the realtors telling them they cannot advertise the right-of-way.

The Captain puts his boat trailer in the right-of-way to discourage any potential buyers.

Captain Troll is ramping up his harassment again. (Here we go !)

Bullies

The oppressed becomes the oppressor.
It is deep rooted in the core of human nature.

The truly ugly side of our species.
A trait only an intelligent being would have, born
of natural instinct.

An emotional flaw fueled by selfishness,
vindictiveness,
greed and anger.

An eye for an eye and tooth for a tooth.
Humans are worse than any other animal on the
planet to act in this way.

The blood of revenge tastes oh so sweet,
it is
addictive to the mind and toxic to the soul.

Mudflap has acquired a taste for the luscious
nectar.
But he is really trying to quit !

Over and Out !

I thought about going on a rant about bullies
during part of a chapter. At 3 a.m. as I woke, I
realized it had to be a chapter all its own.

Throughout history man has been plagued by
bullies, no better example than the Grand Inquisitor.

Born from the need to survive and dominate,

bullying became a warped conception of that need.

There are different degrees of bullying in the animal kingdom. It's part of the survival of the fittest. It seems the more highly developed the intellect, the more likely the bullying. Orcas are a good example of a highly intelligent animal. When they were in captivity in Sea World, two bullied another. The bullied one, the oppressed, later turned his wrath upon a trainer, killing her and becoming the oppressor.

A horrible chain of events, brought on in sequence by a reaction to negative behavior.

The reverse idea of compassion and good behavior would obviously produce a better outcome.

But no animal takes bullying to the level that the human species does. We are the most cruel and vicious of any animal on the planet.

This fact we should recognize so that we can try to make it better. It is an issue of the times, and we are making progress. As much as we want to achieve the goal of no more bullies, sadly that's just not going to happen. At least we are recognizing it in our schools and, hopefully, work places, and we are starting to try.

Before I go on about everyone else, I would like to address Mudflap.

We know Mudflap was bullied from the start by

his brother. His third grade teacher in the Brewster school acted as a tag team player, taking up the slack during the day when the brother was unavailable. A happy memory of that school was playing the May Pole Dance, a tradition I think has all but faded away.

In the next school, named Corn, grades four through six, Mudflap was bullied by a team: three regular classmates and a real big guy. The big guy had stayed back so many times he was being pushed ahead. He was taller and leaner than Mudflap's brother. His arms longer too. Nobody messed with him, and he was always first pick in any basketball game. The three boys recruited the big guy, a fun game of bully was on their minds. Mudflap doesn't blame the big guy, he was just along for the fun. The three would push around Mudflap, distracting him from looking back. The big guy would kneel down on all fours, and as the other boys pushed Mudflap backwards and over the kneeling giant, he would stand up and Mudflap would go flying.

This game was regular business for a while at recess time.

One at a time Mudflap caught each boy alone, and enjoyed his first sips of the sweet nectar revenge.

They eventually stopped their game; it now had consequence.

Mudflap never messed with the big guy, and neither did anyone else. Coincidentally, the big guy lived in the old neighborhood, down by Craze's end of the street.

(I think the ghost of Mrs. Vance is in my spell check. It stops helping me if I keep getting the same word wrong.)

Ah, but the oppressed becomes the oppressor.

Around the same time in the Corn school, Mudflap bullied a boy. He is not really sure now what his reasons were. They have faded away, so it could not have been anything too important, or well deserved.

Mudflap would now like to say to that boy, that he is very, very sorry. And he hopes he is a happy man and has a good life.

Back at our history: There have been many bullies, but in our generation we recognize no one more despicable than Hitler. There is only one reason half the world's most dominant language is not German, and the other half is not Japanese.

Hitler made the mistake of picking on a bigger bully than he realized. The simple short story is that had Stalin not thrown the whole might of his people at Hitler, with a brutal bully vengeance, and disregard for the lives he was sacrificing, the United States wouldn't have acted in time and the world as we know it would have been lost.

Bullies commonly make the mistake of underestimating the focus of their wrath.

The world's a scary place because good does not always prevail.

Mudflap's first wife was the victim of violence. The first thing she did when given a little power, a power given to her to protect her interest, was to abuse that power.

There have been lots of bullies in Mudflap's life, besides fist fights and scrabbles back when Mudflap was a minor. I will pick this one example, because he should have known better. The rest I will lump together in one long sentence.

Back one day when Mudflap's boy was in middle school, the phone rang. It was a gentleman asking for Mr. Mudflap - another coincidence of sorts, because Mudflap was rarely ever at home this early in the day.

He introduced himself as the principal of the school and he had very distressing news for Mudflap. A couple of boys, two real bad characters, had stolen property belonging to Mudflap's son. This graphing calculator was stolen maliciously, and these boys had to be arrested for the crime. He went on to say because the property was actually that of the Mudflaps, that Mr. Mudflap himself had to be the one to press the charges.

Mudflap was taken aback. His first instinct was the defense of his son. He said, "If these kids are such bad characters, my son could get beat up. If not on school grounds, maybe even at the local movie

house. If we are the ones who push the arrest my
son could be hurt. I'm not comfortable with it, sorry
no."

        The Principal was not taking no for an answer,
and went on saying someone had to take a stand,
and that someone should be Mudflap. He went on for
a long time, it was falling on Mudflap's deaf side.
Mudflap held his ground, and finally he stopped,
still sounding frustrated, ending the conversation.

        When the son got home, Mudflap questioned
him. Turns out the son inadvertently left the
calculator in class. The son was embarrassed and
had no intention of telling Mudflap he had been so
careless. He had planned to pay for a new calculator
out of his own savings.

        Next thing you know the state police are
calling. (Here we go!)

        The principal wanted them to put the pressure
on Mudflap to press charges. As much as Mudflap
likes troopers, he is not the type to be sold on
everybody, and true to Connecticut, he was skeptical.
The conversation went the same way as before.

        His impression was this particular cop had it
out for the kid in question, and together with the
principal, they were ganging up. The two kids in
question were no more than 13 to 15 years old.

        When a child is arrested, the whole family is
arrested, drawing everybody into the juvenile

correction system.

     Mudflap, as we all know, is a hard-riding fella who had been through a lot in his lifetime. (The switch flipped !)

     Mudflap didn't like the principal or the cop. They both demanded that something had to be done. Someone had to show discipline!   In that fact Mudflap was in complete agreement, except not exactly the kind of discipline they had in mind.

     The principal's job was to discipline the children. He wanted Mudflap to do his job for him. Mudflap already had a job and did not have the time to do the principal's job too.

     Plus one other little fact, Mudflap knew exactly what it was like to be one of those kids in question.

     The switch flipped all right, and the high beams were on! That principal was the deer in the headlights!

     The principal was safe in the academic world, all neat and tidy. He thought he could just reach out into the real world. Just snap his fingers, stomp his foot, and he would get his way, unchallenged!

     So into the real world he went and rolled over a rock, expecting to find a gold coin. Instead he found a rattlesnake, and it jumped up and bit him faster than he could have ever imagined.

I am going to spare you and myself the eight-page letter and all that went into the research that Mudflap ended up putting together. I will try to put it all as simply and as accurately as I can, without the need for another book.

Mudflap went to the Superintendent and laid out his case. And to the Board of Education, stating clearly the many facts he had put together. The Principal was not only, not doing his job, but was hurting the boys' future.

Once they were booked as criminals, the boys would no longer qualify for the technical school. The trade schools were not looking to pick up the discipline problems from the public schools. Later arrests could damage chances in military careers. The harassment to the boys was sending them down a bad path, all they needed was a little good discipline. The principal didn't want to bother doing the job he was being paid for.

The Board of Education, after a review of the long document Mudflap comprised, said Mudflap had a lot of very valid points. There was only one problem, they couldn't get rid of him even if they wanted to - he was tenured, untouchable. They even had a teacher they had fired for very good reasons, and that teacher had sued them and was collecting money.

The Board of Education's hands were tied.

Mudflap had a meeting with the Superintendent

and the Principal. At the meeting they all discussed the facts at hand. The Principal, still defiant, said, "So what do you want out of all of this?"

One of Mudflap's biggest issues was the record they were trying to place on the children - a dirty record, hurting them.

Mudflap offered him more than the Principal offered the children.

Channeling history Mudflap went on. When the German General Rommel was implicated in a plot against Hitler, they offered him death and the death of his family, or suicide and dignity and to be buried as a hero.

The Superintendent knew where Mudflap was going with this - she had not clued the Principal in – and she wanted to see his reaction to Mudflap and his offer.

The Principal asked, "What are you talking about?"

Mudflap said, "If you leave now, get a new job, I offer you your dignity, which is more than you offered the children."

The Principal said, "Are you mad?"

Mudflap went on to tell him, "I am going to the villagers, we are lighting the torches."

Before Mudflap could continue, the Principal burst up from his chair and exclaimed, "You want me to resign?" And looked at the Superintendent, and exclaimed again, "You knew what he wanted, didn't you?"

In a major hissy fit, the Principal left the room.

Mudflap and the Superintendent stayed a while and chatted (they had become friends through past meetings). She had at first laughed at Mudflap and said he had no chance. Long before he talked to the Board of Education.

She smiled and said, "Well, you tried." Mudflap said, "It's not over."

The next move Mudflap made was to go to the parents of the number one child in question.

From what the bad trooper had told him, he expected to find a couple of folks on the porch with a bottle of whisky and a shotgun across their lap.

They were a very nice couple, with a few kids, and lots of problems on their plate, one being some health issues the mom was fighting. Mudflap showed them all the letters he had been putting together. They sat and read them in awe.

Mudflap didn't really have the time for all this, but his next stop was going to be the PTA, the villagers, and the torches. He already had his torch lit, shovel in hand, Mudflap was on a roll.

A couple days later Mudflap got a call from the Superintendent, who congratulated him. The Principal had found another job and had resigned.

Mudflap did what the Board of Education, the Superintendent and whole system could not.

Mudflap alone fired the Principal.

Later Mudflap was told how the break he gave that boy changed his path, and his life took a whole new turn. He hears today that boy has a family, works very hard and is successful, and is a happy, good man.

The Principal got another principal gig, next few towns over. After a few years, Mudflap heard he left, does not know why. All Mudflap knows, he left his school system with dignity.

Every time Mudflap helped anyone by loaning them money or co-signing to help them, every time without exception, including his own son, they all used that power given them to abuse Mudflap.

I guess that includes everyone, up to date that is.

Mudflap gets the revenge thing: it's an understandable act, regardless of its low moral caliber.

He doesn't get this mass murder epidemic we have of senseless violence. As a gun owner and

NRA member, (it's required to be an NRA member to be in his gun club) Mudflap is completely for background checks.

Most NRA members are pro background checks from what Mudflap understands. (So what's up with that NRA?)

Mudflap doesn't really like algebra, but let's do some for fun. If the entire country's population is X. A much smaller percentage of that population is in the NRA, and we will call them Y. And a tiny percent of the NRA that opposes background checks is Y2. In a democracy where we all get a vote, and the majority rules, how can Y2 control the laws of X?

Background checks do not abolish the Second Amendment. If anything it strengthens it, so the anti-gun people have less to complain about. How is this small percent of the NRA able to bully the whole country?

Gee, I almost forgot the Puritans escaping religious persecution. They turned around and did the same thing to others.

Mudflap has always been a proud New Englander, proud he had family back as far as the Mayflower. His father had paperwork, something about being in the Sons and Daughters of the American Revolution. With the poor connection he had with his father, Mudflap was not interested at the time. But he always thought it was cool he had that Mayflower connection.

Once Mudflap found out what the pilgrims did, he was no longer proud. After their numbers grew, they began a war on the very people that saved them in the beginning.

There is some island off the coast of India, somewhere. The natives will kill anyone who lands on their island. Mudflap thinks they have the right idea. The Native Americans should have done the same thing, and if they did, they would still have their country.

On a personal level: Mudflap cannot figure out the motive, or the over-blown ego of the big bully Captain Troll.

That's Mudflap's rant on bullies.

Over and Out !

Wrap Up

You cannot control the actions of others, you can only control your own actions.

That's a quote from Mudflap's sweet, little, introverted wife.

**She feels it is not only her job, but her duty to point out any
and all of Mudflap's faults.**

Mudflap, Over and Out !

Summer vacation is over, the end of August is still hot, but it's on the wind-down. Mudflap is relieved to be back. It seems all he's been doing is hustling around. He has not gained a pound from having the time off.

Daughter is sporting a new boyfriend. They all had a good bonding on the island hop. Mudflap did get a few books read. They are the only things that slowed down the time, and gave Mudflap any real escape.

Mudflap's hernia is hurting more all the time. It's actually feeling better at work. Lugging the water, fuel, docking equipment and gear had increased the swelling a lot. He is becoming more conscious of diet playing a part in the pain as well.

Mudflap and friend get through the first month of work. It's been a rainy season and it's still not letting up.

End of September was the last work trip to Maine. They close the camps up, slip past the Troll as quickly as possible, and were gone. Both islands are on the market, but the season's wrapping up fast, looks like it's not going to happen this year.

As soon as the season ends for the islands, planning for next season begins.

Captain Troll does not like Mudflap's dock, and wants him to take it down every time the family leaves.

Mudflap, now in his sixties, is planning to be at Phoebe Island more all the time. Taking down the dock every time he leaves is not going to work anymore. (Mudflap has a plan.)

Mudflap got a great idea from his carpenter buddy in Naples. You can get used aluminum wheelchair ramps cheap once people pass on or go to assisted living. They are the perfect size to use as docks. The rails and platforms fit the material specifications well for Phoebe Island. Mudflap and his wife will be able to go out safely in their later years.

The Mudflaps are in their sixties. The later years are here now.

It's the fall of 2018; Mudflap has been running around and has acquired five sets of ramps before the first snowfall. He is ready for spring.

Mudflap took the Phoebe Island off the market because the season was almost over and the trouble with Captain Troll's harassment being on the upswing, again.

When Mudflap puts up his new dock, much bigger than the ramps he uses now, the Troll is not going to like it.

Is Captain Troll going to go "Bully Crazy" on Mudflap?

Is Mudflap going to get buried up by the pond with Ellie the pup?

Is the Captain looking for a boat ride up the state river, for the rest of his summers with "Bubba" ?

Is Mudflap going to get to finish his work at Pine Island?

Is this story turning into a cliffhanger?

All this is on Mudflap's mind.

November is almost here and the Old Tree Cutter ponders his life, and his future.

He starts joking around with his wife and daughter calling himself Mudflap because he feels like he's under the bus so much that he lives there.

He starts to relate the Mudflap feelings to some of his clients who have kids the same age as Mudflap's. They feel it too and know exactly where he is coming from.

He starts to tease his daughter, leaving messages on her phone and at the end of the message the last thing he would say is: Mudflap, over and out!

Mudflap was talking to a client he has worked with for 25 years or more. This particular man is a well-respected professional, and had a very large and completely unfair judgment put against him. He is the nicest guy and did not deserve all the aggravation. They have children about the same age. Mudflap told him that he felt he was under the bus all the time. His reply was exactly what Mudflap had told his wife. He exclaimed, "I live under the bus!"

Mudflap knew then he was really on to something - he was not alone, not at all.

It's almost Thanksgiving time, Mudflap's wife hands him a letter. It's from his son. Mudflap has been leaving his son alone, giving him space. With the holidays approaching fast, Mudflap is glad to get the letter. He is expecting it to read something like: I have been busy at work and with the new wife. We haven't had any time together, so let's hit the club in the New Year and get some target practice in. I will take you to lunch after, just like the old days.

Mudflap opened up the letter, after the first

sentence he put it down. He looks at his wife and says, "This is a complete pile of crap." He takes a couple of deep breaths and trudges through the rest of the letter to its horrible, bitter conclusion.

The letter is so bad that it is actually a relief to Mudflap. He has been taking all the blame for the trouble with his son. Of course the boy's mom has been on the boy's side the whole time, giving Mudflap all the heat.

Wife and mother could no longer blame Mudflap for everything. The content of the letter was just too off the wall, even for her to defend.

The whole holiday season had a damper put on it.

Mudflap's bigger concern is the surgery he was facing come January 21st.

In his time Mudflap has had some serious injuries: knee, shoulder, and back. But he was never cut open, and never missed work either. He relentlessly pounded through the rain and snow with the injuries plaguing him all the way.

His mom died after a surgery trying to correct irritable bowel syndrome. The syndrome was created by medicine given to the mom earlier for something completely unrelated, the side effect of the medicine being the syndrome itself.

Mudflap witnessed his mother being butchered

in the hospital, and was terrified to have any surgery at all, especially on his gut.

As the days clicked closer to the surgery, Mudflap became increasingly anxious.

A close friend and client, a sweet lady Mudflap is very fond of, had been through a very hard time and a few nasty surgeries. As she faced one of her surgeries she confided in Mudflap and told him, with a bit of a tear, but with a stiff upper lip, that she felt it was the end for her.

Mudflap gave all the love he could to her, and told her things were going to be all right. I must say it's an easier thing to say when you're not the one facing the operating table.

Mudflap's friend beat her illness and recovered from the surgery well. As Mudflap's surgery date closed in, his friend was now comforting him saying everything was going to go well. Mudflap was not facing what she had faced, he was being a baby compared to her. That helped Mudflap a lot.

Mudflap had to put off people needing service. Everyone was very kind and supportive, helping Mudflap face the date coming closer and closer.

Once the surgery takes place Mudflap will be out of commission for 12 weeks. He worked doing every tree job he could as well as chores around his house and shop. He pushed himself hard right to the last day, doing all he could.

Mudflap's wife had to deal with his anxiety - he can be trouble enough anyway - but now he's really not a happy camper.

It's Monday the 21st, Mudflap has to be at Hartford Hospital by 5 a.m.

Mudflap and wife drive over the mountain in the tail wind of a snow storm, riding in the light of the Full Super Wolf Moon.

Mudflap is processed, and is wheeled into the O.R.

The crew and surgeon were happy, all smiles. Mudflap was not happy at all, but relieved to see the crew pumped up and positive.

He was almost ok until they swapped him over to the narrow little table. Then the wings came out like the execution table you see on TV.

Now he was freaking out, his last thoughts of consciousness were that of his baby girl.

He did wake up, and that's a good thing.

His surgeon was upbeat, happy with his good work. He told Mudflap he had cut it real close, his large intestine and appendix ready to blow through.

Mudflap cut it real close working himself right to the edge of his limits.

Picture perfect, in true Mudflap style.

He got home and tried to relax, one more hurdle to go.

They told him before the surgery he might need to go back to the hospital for a catheter.

He was never so happy to pee in his whole life.

The next day his wife helped him up and around the house, and made him one of her super-sized extra cheese omelets.

He went back to bed with his laptop and started writing that book he had been thinking about.

The hernia didn't get him, but now it was time to spill his guts.

His first thoughts were that of his baby girl's statement.

"No matter what you do, daddy, you will always be under the bus."

Mudflap, Over and Out !

Epilogue

When Bob Bailey took dynamite to the Great Hill Pond Dam, he altered the course of events for himself and everyone in his family.

That action turned their lives upside down and forever ruined the proper connection and influence he would have with his sons.

He forever changed the dynamics of his family and for generations to come.

Acknowledgements

I acknowledge all the unnamed people in my book and life, good and bad, who made me who I am today.

With special thanks to:

My daughter Alexandra and wife Martha without whom it would be at all worthwhile.

And:

David Attenborough, whose voice and series I like very much.

Leslie Buck, fellow arborist and author.

Vincent, at La Rosa Construction, for the dam gate information.

And, last but not least,

Aesop the Philosopher, and *The Rocky and Bullwinkle Show.*